FRAGMENTS

of

HOLINESS

For Daily Reflection

Edited by
CATHERINE ROBINSON

The Lindsey Press
LONDON

Published by The Lindsey Press
on behalf of The General Assembly of Unitarian
and Free Christian Churches
Essex Hall, 1–6 Essex Street,
London, WC2R 3HY, UK

© The General Assembly of Unitarian
and Free Christian Churches 2019

ISBN 978-0-85319-091-2

Designed and typeset by Bryony Clark
Chapter ornaments: Shutterstock.com

We receive fragments of holiness,
glimpses of eternity, brief moments of insight.
Let us gather them up for the precious gifts that they are,
and, renewed by their grace, move boldly into the unknown.

SARAH YORK
Unitarian Universalist minister

(From *Into the Wilderness*, Apollo Ranch Institute Press, 2nd edition, 2000)

CONTENTS

Preface   vi

JANUARY   1

FEBRUARY   16

MARCH   31

APRIL   46

MAY   60

JUNE   75

JULY   91

AUGUST   107

SEPTEMBER   124

OCTOBER   139

NOVEMBER   157

DECEMBER   173

Sources   191
Index of authors   202

PREFACE

Fragments of Holiness is a collection of reflective texts for every day of the year which I hope readers will find inspiring and challenging. It is, admittedly, a very personal selection (mostly mine, but with contributions by fellow members of the Lindsey Press Panel, David Dawson and Reverend Claire MacDonald, and several other pieces suggested by friends and by members of my own Unitarian congregation in Oxford).

More than half the texts are the work of Unitarians or Unitarian Universalists, past and present, famous or unknown. Almost one quarter present insights from world faiths, ranging from Christian mystics to an anonymous Zoroastrian. The rest come from a multitude of sources, including humanist philosophers, radical social activists, and world literature.

Of the Unitarian and Unitarian Universalist sources, Ralph Waldo Emerson and his fellow Transcendentalists are well represented, but the most frequently quoted source is A. Powell Davies (1902–1957). He was a Welshman who emigrated to the United States, led Unitarian congregations in New Jersey and Washington DC, opposed the House Un-American Activities Committee, and campaigned for civil rights and women's rights. Powell Davies' preaching style was uniquely poetical. It was the following insight (quoted in this anthology) that led me 25 years ago to realise that I am a Unitarian: *'There is no God in the sky. God is in the heart that loves the sky's blueness.'*

This collection is offered primarily as a resource for private devotions. You might like to use it as part of a daily practice of contemplation, at the start or the end of the day; or – if, like me, you are lucky enough to be retired from full-time employment – half-way through the morning with a cup of coffee, sitting at a window and enjoying the sky's blueness. But it could also be used as a resource for group contemplation and discussion. Reverend Kate Dean (minister of the Rosslyn Hill Unitarian Chapel) suggests a form of 'lectio divina': the members of the group undertake to read one week's worth of texts in advance (for a weekly meeting) or one month's worth (for a monthly meeting). Kate explains: "Light a candle and start with a time of silent reflection. Then the members take turns to read aloud their favourite text, sharing thoughts about how it resonates (or not) with their own experience, and the implications for their own lives. Some of the shorter readings could be written out by hand to prompt ten minutes of 'freewriting' (stream-of-consciousness composition), followed by a discussion of the results."

Unitarian preachers in search of opening or closing words for their services might also find this collection useful, especially as many of the entries commemorate notable dates in our long history.

In whatever way the book is used, I hope that it will be in the spirit of these beautiful words by Sarah York, a retired Unitarian Universalist minister:

> *We receive fragments of holiness,*
> *glimpses of eternity, brief moments of insight.*
> *Let us gather them up for the precious gifts that they are,*
> *and, renewed by their grace, move boldly into the unknown.*

My thanks are due to Sarah for permission to use her words – and my thanks, too, to all the other writers who are represented in this collection.

Catherine Robinson
Oxford, January 2019

A NOTE FOR NON-UNITARIAN READERS

The Unitarian movement has evolved over 400 years from a heretical Protestant sect into a liberal religious community, imposing no creed, and open to people of all faiths and none. The name reflects a belief in the oneness of God and the essential unity of all humankind and all creation.

The historical roots of Unitarianism are in Christianity, but the founders were branded as heretics because they regarded Jesus of Nazareth as a human prophet rather than a divine being. Although we try to live by his moral teaching, we don't believe that Christianity has a monopoly on the truth, so we are free to seek inspiration from a wide range of sources, and our congregations include humanists, atheists, and agnostics as well as people with more theistic beliefs. We meet to celebrate the beauty of the earth and the human potential for goodness; to open our minds to new insights from philosophers, poets, and all the great world faiths; to share our joys and concerns with each other; and to seek inspiration to lead better lives.

More information can be found at www.unitarian.org.uk.

JANUARY

January 1st

As we look back on the year that has ended, each of us can probably recall a friend or family member whom we have lost. At this season of renewal and new hope, let us take a few moments to think about loss, and how precious and precarious all things are. Let's take one good look at the passingness of things, the precious fragility of everything. A single blade of grass, a much-loved coffee mug, a fading photograph, a quick kiss: all speak of the wonder and transitoriness of life-and-death. There is beauty and wonder in this existence. And the simple truth is that this very moment is the only place where we will find life and love and meaning.[1]

JAMES ISHMAEL FORD
Zen Buddhist priest and retired Unitarian Universalist minister

January 2nd

The past is past; we cannot alter it now; that book is closed. It gave us many things to be glad about, and we are grateful. It gave us other things which were cause for sorrow and repentance; and we are truly sorry. But only the future is free. Humbly we accept the gift of unused minutes and hours and days and years, praying that we may use them rightly.[2]

HARRY LISMER SHORT
1906–1975, Unitarian Principal of Manchester College Oxford

January 3rd

Our lives move in one direction, there is no going back. May joy be ours on the journey; joy in sharing it with those who share the Way. However long the road, however hard, help us, amidst the tears, always to find reasons for laughter, song, and praise as we travel together. May it be so.[3]

CLIFF REED
Unitarian minister, retired

January 4th

Universal Spirit of love, O God within each one of us,
whose power reaches to the stars, whose love connects
us one to another and to all creation – we are one. …
We give thanks for the blessings of love in our lives and
for the chance we have to love again and always. May we
feel the love inside us connecting with the love in each
other and the stars.[4]

DOROTHY MAY EMERSON
Unitarian Universalist minister

January 5th

God is the fact of the fact, the life of the life, the soul
   of the soul,
the incomprehensible, the sum of all contradictions,
the unity of all diversity. …
God cannot be seen, but by God all seeing comes;
cannot be heard, yet by him all hearing comes.
Turn your back upon God and you turn your back
upon gravity, upon air, upon light.
God is not a being, yet apart from God there is no being.
There is no apart from God.[5]

JOHN BURROUGHS
1837–1921, American naturalist

January 6th

People may flatter themselves just as much by thinking
that their faults are always present to other people's
minds, as if they believe that the world is always
contemplating their individual charms and virtues.

ELIZABETH GASKELL
Unitarian novelist, 1810–1865

January 7th

Teach us, good lord, that being religious consists not in
the observation of holy days but in the living of holy lives,
for each day provides us with a golden opportunity for
doing good. And help us to see the folly of yearning after
eternity when we have not yet learned to use wisely the
few short hours of a single day.[6]

JOHN ANDREW STOREY
1935–1997, Unitarian minister

January 8th

Expect Life! Do not live too far in the past or the future;
live now.

In each moment expect a miracle: ten kinds of birds
at the feeder, and the tracks of a fox in the snow.

Run naked through the garden early in the morning
and hope the wild geese fly by.

Get silly and laugh with your grandchildren, or your

grandparents. Refuse to leave the dead behind, but bring their memory to all your chores and games and corners of quiet warm tears.

Know always that joy and sorrow are woven together; one cannot be without the other. If you love, know that sometimes your love will bring you tears; if you grieve, know it is because at some time you were willing to love.

Do not be afraid to die today. But expect life![7]

ELIZABETH TARBOX
1944–1999, Unitarian Universalist minister

January 9th

Do not be daunted by the enormity of the world's grief. Do justly, now. Love mercy, now. Walk humbly, now. You are not obligated to complete the work, but neither are you free to abandon it.

RABBI TARFON
c. 70 CE–135 CE

January 10th

You say grace before meals. All right. But I say grace before the concert and the opera, and grace before the play and pantomime, and grace before I open a book, and grace before sketching, painting, swimming, walking, playing, and dancing – and grace before I dip my pen in the ink.[8]

G.K. CHESTERTON
1874–1936, Catholic writer, Unitarian parents

January 11th

Know first who you are and what you are capable of. …
We are always learning, always growing. It is right to accept
challenges. This is when we progress to the next level of
intellectual, physical, or moral development. Still, do not
deceive yourself: if you try to be something or someone
you are not, you belittle your true self and end up not
developing in those areas that you would have excelled in
quite naturally. Within the divine order we each have our
own special calling. Listen to yours, and follow it faithfully.

EPICTETUS
Greek Stoic philosopher, 55–135 CE

January 12th

God is what the soul affirms when life is accepted – all
of it; the pain of it; the complications; the tortured hour
of decision; yes, and the tragedy and greatness of a time
like this. When the soul says, I will live in this time, live
in it and for it and beyond it; live out its truth at any
cost, live for its justice waiting to be done, live for its
beauty trampled underfoot; live for its tenderness, its
compassion, its love, which multitudes are doubting and
other multitudes have cast away; when the soul says, I
accept the life that is given me, the joy of it and the pain
of it; I accept it and affirm it, and I will do what is given
me to do; that is belief in God.[9]

A. POWELL DAVIES
1902–1957, Unitarian minister

January 13th

God be in my head, and in my understanding;
God be in mine eyes, and in my looking;
God be in my mouth, and in my speaking;
God be in my heart, and in my thinking;
God be at mine end, and at my departing.

THE SARUM PRIMER

1514

January 14th

The ethic of reverence for life is the ethic of Jesus brought
to philosophical expression, extended into cosmic form,
and conceived as intellectually necessary.[10]

ALBERT SCHWEITZER

*1875–1965, philosopher, musician, and doctor; member of the Unitarian
Universalist Church of the Larger Fellowship, born on this day*

January 15th

All life is interrelated. We are caught in an inescapable
network of mutuality; tied in a single garment of destiny.
Whatever affects one directly affects all indirectly. As long
as there is poverty in this world, no man can be totally
rich, even if he has a billion dollars. As long as diseases
are rampant and millions of people cannot expect to live
more than twenty or thirty years, no man can be totally
healthy, even if he just got a clean bill of health from the

finest clinic in America. Strangely enough, I can never be
what I ought to be until you are what you ought to be.
You can never be what you ought to be until I am what I
ought to be.[11]

MARTIN LUTHER KING JR.
1929–1968, civil-rights leader, born on this day

January 16th

Do not attach yourself to any particular creed
exclusively, so that you disbelieve all the rest … God,
the omnipresent and omnipotent, is not limited to one
creed, for He says "Wherever you turn, there is the face
of Allah". (Qur'an 2:115)

IBN AL-ARABI
1165–1240, Sufi mystic, poet, and philosopher

The lamps are different, but the light is the same.

JALAL UL-DIN RUMI
1207–1273, poet, scholar, theologian, Sufi mystic

January 17th

Love your enemies, for they tell you your faults.

BENJAMIN FRANKLIN
Unitarian President of the USA, 1706–1790, born on this day

January 18th

The Love of God
The Peace of God
The Warmth of God
The Surprise of God
The Completeness of God
Be among us and within us
Now and forever. Amen.[12]

January 19th

No one is born hating another person because of the colour of his skin, or his background, or his religion. People must learn to hate, and if they can learn to hate, they can be taught to love, for love comes more naturally to the human heart than its opposite.[13]

NELSON MANDELA
1918–2013, anti-apartheid leader,
President of South Africa from 1994 to 1999

January 20th

Let us remember and enfold with our love those in trouble of any kind; those worse off than we are in any respect; those who cannot cope on their own. Let us take time in quietness now to share with God those particular concerns that we hold in our hearts, believing that remembering, that caring, that loving will help in time of need. ... May we commit ourselves again, in our own hearts and minds, to the service and the doing of truth and love, in the ways which lie closest to us: loving one another, and the divinity in each other, accepting and serving others in their need.[14]

BRUCE FINDLOW
Unitarian minister, Principal of Manchester College Oxford 1974–1985

January 21st

If your paid employment is a vexation to your spirit, or if you have no paid employment, there is still meaningful work for you to do. You can find a way to volunteer your time and talent for the benefit of others. You can indulge a creative urge, grow things, get involved in the political process. Meaningful work connects you to that which transcends and abides. Meaningful work is about more than the accumulation of wealth, power or status, or about finding something to do to fill the days. It is a key step towards spiritual health. There is no shortage of such work to be done, regardless of the state of the jobs market or the economy, and no lack of different ways in which it might be performed.[15]

DAVID USHER
Unitarian minister

January 22nd

My Symphony

To live content with small means; to seek elegance rather
   than luxury, and refinement rather than fashion;
to be worthy, not respectable, and wealthy, not rich;
to study hard, think quietly, talk gently, act frankly;
to listen to stars and birds, to babes and sages, with an
   open heart;
to hear all cheerfully, do all bravely, await occasions,
   hurry never.
In a word, to let the spiritual, unbidden, and unconscious
   grow up through the commonplace.
This is to be my symphony.

WILLIAM ELLERY CHANNING (THE YOUNGER)
1818–1901, Unitarian minister, nephew of Unitarian theologian
William Ellery Channing, who died in 1842

January 23rd

We have to be born again and again and again and again
until we die.

UNNAMED UNITARIAN MINISTER
quoted in The Inquirer, *16 November 2017*

January 24th

If you were to live three thousand years, or even thirty thousand, remember that the sole life that you can lose is that which you are living at the moment; and furthermore, that you can have no other life except the one that you lose. This means that the longest life and the shortest life amount to the same thing. For the passing minute is every person's equal possession, but what has once gone by is not ours. Our loss, therefore, is limited to that one fleeting instant, since no one can lose what is already past, nor yet what is still to come – for how can we be deprived of what we do not possess?[16]

MARCUS AURELIUS
Stoic philosopher and Emperor of Rome from 161 to 180 CE

January 25th

Every man I meet is my superior in some way, and in that I learn of him.

RALPH WALDO EMERSON
1803–1882, Unitarian minister, essayist, and philosopher,
Boston, Massachusetts

January 26th

Take a moment to think of all the strangers you meet in your own life in a typical week: folk working in shops, in libraries, the garage attendant, strangers on trains, or people standing with you at the bus stop. How would it be if each of us took a couple of minutes this week to chat to someone we meet and just listen to what they have to say? Just listen. It's a very modest notion, but who knows how much good it might do that person to be listened to, and how much good it might do us to listen?[17]

MATTHEW SMITH
Unitarian minister, Bury St Edmunds and Framlingham

January 27th
Holocaust Memorial Day

Monsters exist, but they are too few in number to be truly dangerous. More dangerous are the common men, the functionaries ready to believe and to act without asking questions.[18]

PRIMO LEVI
1919–1987, writer, chemist, Auschwitz survivor

January 28th

Sit quietly. For a minute or so, concentrate on your breathing. Look at a tree. Greet it as you would a stranger, or, if you know it well, as an old friend. … Observe its physical structure, its various colours, the texture of its bark, and the shapes and hues of its leaves and branches. … Now consider the silent interior, the unseen energies and processes which prompted it to grow from a tiny seed, and which enable it to convert water and mineral salts into such living beauty. And say to youself quietly: "Don't nobody know why".[19]

BILL DARLISON
Unitarian minister, retired

January 29th

What do we really mean by the term 'nonviolence'? In combat you may risk your life to kill others; in nonviolence you may risk your life so that no one else will be killed. This requires rigorous training and deep conviction; the effect it has on violent, cruel, or angry people is *more powerful than more violence*. It affects them at a profound level. It is the force of Satyagraha, developed by Gandhi and entirely successful in driving the British out of India. The practitioner renounces the use of force, voluntarily and on principle, and replaces it with determination combined with compassion, combined with courage.[20]

SCILLA ELWORTHY
International peace campaigner

January 30th

It is the action, not the fruit of the action, that is important. You have to do the right thing. It may not be in your power, may not be in your time, that there will be fruit, but that doesn't mean you stop doing the right thing. You may never know what results come from your action. But if you do nothing, there will be no result.

MAHATMA GANDHI
1869–1948, Indian independence leader, assassinated on this day

January 31st

How does it happen in this poor world that You are so near, yet nobody finds You? That in all things You speak, yet nobody hears You? That Your signature is everywhere in the beauty of things, yet nobody knows Your name? We close our eyes, and say we cannot see You, we stop our ears, and say we cannot hear. We flee from You, and say we cannot find You. Present always, You are nearer to us than we are to ourselves – but too often WE are not there.[21]

JACOB TRAPP
1899–1992, Unitarian Universalist minister

FEBRUARY

*February 1st**

If the stars should appear one night in a thousand
years, how would men believe and adore; and preserve
for many generations the remembrance of the city of
God which had been shown! But every night come out
these envoys of beauty, and light the universe with their
admonishing smile.

RALPH WALDO EMERSON
1803–1882, Unitarian minister, essayist, and philosopher, Massachusetts

* Laurel Salton Clark, a Unitarian Universalist, died on this day in
2003 with six other astronauts when their spaceship Colombia
disintegrated, 39 miles above the Earth.

February 2nd

O God, give me light in my heart and light in my tongue and light in my hearing and light in my sight and light in my feeling and light in all my body and light before me and light behind me. Give me, I pray, light on my right hand and light on my left and light above me and light beneath me. O Lord, increase light within me and give me light and illuminate me.

Ascribed to THE PROPHET MUHAMMAD

February 3rd

At some stage we must let go of the past and begin again. No one is undeserving of forgiveness – and that includes you. I know it can be difficult to offer ourselves the forgiveness that we can so freely give to others. Perhaps we hold ourselves to a higher standard than the standard to which we hold other people – but let's admit that this double standard is actually a piece of arrogance: "I am a better person than he or she is, so I should behave better." None among us should be defined as the sum total of our worst actions. None of us is a monster. We are all fragile and flawed humans who commit offences against others. When we do these things, we are not monsters; we are human beings who have become separated from our own goodness.[22]

DESMOND TUTU
Former Archbishop of Cape Town

February 4th
Rosa Parks Day

At the time I was arrested I had no idea it would turn into this. It was just a day like any other day. The only thing that made it significant was that the masses of the people joined in.[23]

ROSA PARKS

1913–2005, arrested in Montgomery, Alabama, in 1955
for refusing to give up her seat on a bus to a white man

February 5th

A hypocrite is the kind of politician who would cut down a redwood tree, then mount the stump and make a speech for conservation.

ADLAI STEVENSON

Unitarian diplomat and 'universal citizen', 1900–1965, born on this day

February 6th

Divine Spirit, who turns the ordinary into the sacred, be with us in the daily routine and in the mundane. We call to mind the times when we have failed to honour ourselves and others as sacred beings; the times when we have failed to treat the world as a sacred space; the times when we have neglected to look for the sacred aspects of everyday life … and we listen for the still small voice that encourages us to forgive ourselves and begin again.[24]

ANTHONY HOWE
Unitarian minister, Birmingham Hollywood

February 7th

That was a memorable day to me, for it made great changes in me. But it is the same with any life. Imagine one selected day struck out of it, and think how different its course would have been. Pause you who read this, and think for a moment of the long chain of iron or gold, of thorns or flowers, that would never have bound you, but for the formation of the first link on one memorable day.[25]

CHARLES DICKENS
Unitarian author and social reformer, 1812–1870, born on this day

February 8th

All that we ought to have thought and have not thought,
All that we ought to have said, and have not said,
All that we ought to have done, and have not done;

All that we ought not to have thought, and yet have
  thought,
All that we ought not to have spoken, and yet have spoken,
All that we ought not to have done, and yet have done;

For thoughts, words, and works, pray we, O God,
  for forgiveness.

ZOROASTRIAN PRAYER

February 9th

When it can be said by any country in the world that my
poor are happy, neither ignorance nor distress is to be
found among them, my jails are empty of prisoners, my
streets of beggars, the aged are not in want, the taxes are
not oppressive, the rational world is my friend because
I am the friend of happiness. When these things can be
said, then may that country boast its constitution and
government. Independence is my happiness, the world is
my country, and my religion is to do good.[26]

THOMAS PAINE
*1737–1809, political revolutionary, Unitarian connections,
born on this day*

February 10th

I own that I am disposed to say grace upon twenty other occasions in the course of the day besides my dinner. I want a form for setting out upon a pleasant walk, for a moonlight ramble, for a friendly meeting, or a solved problem. Why have none for books, those spiritual repasts – a grace before Milton – a grace before Shakespeare – a devotional exercise proper to be said before reading *The Faerie Queen*? [27]

CHARLES LAMB
1775–1834, Unitarian essayist and poet, born on this day

February 11th

As I walked out of the door towards the gate that would lead to my freedom, I knew if I didn't leave my bitterness and hatred behind, I'd still be in prison. [28]

NELSON MANDELA
1918–2013; President of South Africa, 1994–99,
released on this day in 1990 after 27 years in jail

February 12th

To say that we are the presence of God in this world is not a metaphor. We are the face of God in this world, and God's voice and hands. God changes outcomes in this world only as we change them. God is not an independent agent, in other words. God is dependent upon us. The active agency of the divine life emerges through our choices and actions.[29]

GALEN GUENGERICH
Unitarian Universalist minister

February 13th

They that love beyond the world cannot be separated by it. Death cannot kill what never dies. Nor can spirits ever be divided that love and live in the same divine principle, the root and record of their friendship. ... Death is but crossing the world, as friends do the seas: they live in one another still. For they must needs be present that love and live in that which is omnipresent. ... This is the comfort of friends, that though they may be said to die, yet their friendship and society are, in the best sense, ever present, because immortal.[30]

WILLIAM PENN
1644–1718, Quaker founder of the State of Pennsylvania

February 14th
Valentine's Day

Loving is more than compromise and trade-off; it is mutual nurturing of growth. Loving is more than trust in each other; it is trust in something that transcends human expectation. Love is the mutual gift of freedom with the mutual gift of commitment. Love is more than being true to ourselves; it is being true to a common reverence for life and a common vision of community. Love is more than loving each other; it is loving Life itself.[31]

SARAH YORK
Unitarian Universalist minister

February 15th

Sooner or later we all discover that the important moments in life are not the advertised ones, not the birthdays, the graduations, the weddings, not the great goals achieved. The real milestones are less prepossessing. They come to the door of memory unannounced, stray dogs that amble in, sniff around a bit and simply never leave. Our lives are measured by these.[32]

SUSAN B. ANTHONY
Unitarian and Quaker feminist and social reformer, 1820–1906,
born on this day

February 16th

… Where, then, is God? In the conclusion of some argument? The final clause of some syllogism? No, the God you can argue yourself into finding is a God you can argue yourself into losing. The living God is in the life itself. God is in the miseries of the world waiting to be ended, in the comprehension that only compassionate hearts can achieve. God is with the helpless and forsaken, with those who are waiting for renewed humanity. God is in the ventures, difficult and dangerous, in the truth that too few speak. God is in the justice that is waiting to be done.

A. POWELL DAVIES

1902–1957, Unitarian minister, Washington, DC

February 17th

For the earth we give thanks: may we respect it, enjoy it, and hand it on unspoiled.

For living beings we give thanks: may we reverence them, wonder at them, and share the world with them as best we can.

For children we give thanks: may we love them, guide them, and let them go when the time comes.

For grown-ups we give thanks: may we suffer them, forgive them, and try to do better ourselves.

For ourselves we give thanks: may we know them, confront them, and learn that they are worth loving.

For God we give thanks: whoever, whatever, He, She, or It may be, for without God there would be nothing to give thanks for, nothing to give thanks.[33]

CLIFF REED

Unitarian minister, retired

February 18th

In each day may I structure a time of silence in which
to be reborn. A time to walk beneath the trees and let
the blood surge through my body. A time to sit silently
and rejoice in the overwhelming splendour of life, and
stars, and grass. A time to know I wish to love today:
to greet my friends with thanksgiving, to know life
is too short to indulge in self-pity. May I avoid the
temptation of easy despair, and reach out to at least
one other person today.

RICHARD BOEKE
Unitarian minister, retired

February 19th

Friendship is the inexpressible comfort of feeling safe
with a person, having neither to weigh thoughts nor
measure words.

GEORGE ELIOT (MARY ANN EVANS)
1819–1880; novelist; member of the Rosslyn Hill
Unitarian congregation, Hampstead

The only way to have a friend is to be one.

RALPH WALDO EMERSON
1803–1882, Unitarian minister, essayist, and philosopher,
Boston, Massachusetts

February 20th

May we find the world to be so beautiful, and life so richly and meaningfully shared, that we shall want this to be true, more often, for more people, everywhere.

JACOB TRAPP
1899–1992, Unitarian Universalist minister

February 21st

I have seen a mother at a crib – so I know what love is;
I have looked into the eyes of a child – so I know what faith is;
I have seen a rainbow – so I know what beauty is;
I have felt the pounding of the sea – so I know what power is;
I have planted a tree – so I know what hope is;
I have heard a wild bird sing – so I know what freedom is;
I have seen a chrysalis burst into life – so I know what mystery is;
I have lost a friend – so I know what sorrow is;
I have seen a star-decked sky – so I know what infinity is;
I have seen and felt all these things – so I know what God is.

VON OGDEN VOGT
1879–1964, minister of the First Unitarian Church Chicago

February 22nd

Your task is not to seek for love, but merely to seek all the barriers within yourself that you have built against it.

JALAL UL-DIN RUMI
1207–1273, poet, scholar, theologian, Sufi mystic

February 23rd

To be in union with God is to be in the NOW. When we surrender our attachment to whom we 'think' we are, to whom we have been in the past and who we want to be, or who we fear we will be in the future, with all the anxiety-producing 'if onlys' and 'what ifs', we enter the NOW, a state of true spiritual freedom which opens the door to unconditional Love for ourselves and all beings. … When we gradually learn to be fully in each moment of life as it occurs, there is just this … and then this … and then this. Each moment of life as it occurs is what life is … this is it … this is it … I am. When consciousness is here now, this is the Timeless Moment, the Eternal Now.[34]

DAVID MONK
Unitarian minister, leader of the Meditation Fellowship, died 2011

February 24th

I beseech you, gentlemen, by the grace of God, to think it possible that you may be wrong.

OLIVER CROMWELL

1599–1658, soldier, revolutionary, parliamentarian

The less wisdom one has, the more one holds to one's ideas. In the wisest person there is the willingness to submit to others. And the most foolish person is always ready to stand firm to support his own ideas.

HAZRAT INAYAT KHAN

1882–1927, Sufi Universalist teacher

February 25th

A church whose creed is truth, whose worship is love;
a society full of industry, wisdom, and the poetry of life;
a state with unity among all, with freedom for each.
A church without tyranny, a society without want,
a state without oppression, a world with no war. Shall
this ever become a fact? History says, No. Human nature
says, Yes.[35]

THEODORE PARKER

*1810–1860, Unitarian minister and Transcendentalist
in Boston, Massachusetts*

February 26th

Thank you, God, for filling things:
Filling the world with people,
Filling words with meaning,
Filling life with happenings,
Filling our plates with food,
And our wallets and purses with money.
May we ask one more thing?
Please fill our hearts with thankfulness.

ANONYMOUS

February 27th

What place, if any, does prayer have in the lives of those
who think of God as a Power, rather than a Person? Can
we establish any meaningful relationship with a Deity
that is other than personal? How does one pray to the
Ground of Being? The analogy of electricity may provide
one answer. Electricity is an invisible force, though we
are able to see some of its manifestations. We don't know
exactly what it is, or fully understand how it works, yet by
plugging various appliances into this impersonal force we
are able to obtain heat, light, and power. In like manner,
by 'plugging in' to the great Life Force or Ground of
Being – the creative Cosmic Energy which some call
'God' – we can recharge our spiritual batteries.[36]

JOHN ANDREW STOREY
1935–1997, British Unitarian minister

February 28th

On the death of a friend, we should consider that the fates have devolved on us the task of a double living: that we have henceforth to fulfill the promise of our friend's life also, in our own, to the world.

HENRY DAVID THOREAU
*1817–1862, Transcendentalist poet, philosopher, and naturalist,
raised as a Unitarian, writing in his journal on this day in 1840*

February 29th

If triangles made a god, they would give him three sides.

CHARLES DE MONTESQUIEU
1689–1755, political philosopher

MARCH

March 1st

Life is precious and is a gift. The world is beautiful, and
we are privileged to live in it. May we know this as truth.
And what we know as truth, may we exhibit in our lives.[37]

ANTHONY HOWE
Unitarian minister, Birmingham Hollywood

March 2nd

The board game of Snakes and Ladders was devised as
a metaphor for the living of life. … There are setbacks.
Sliding down a 'snake' literally brings us low, but – in life
as in the game – we must pick ourselves up and carry
on. Sometimes one is given a boost, we are uplifted. The
'ladder' may take us to unexpected places, new areas to
explore or new fields in which to grow. … The last few
squares are free of either snakes or ladders. The last bit

of the journey must be travelled on one's own. But more
than that: it may be a time of waiting, because one cannot
leave the 'board' until one throws the exact number on
the dice to finish. We never know how many throws of
the dice we have left.[38]

ALISON THURSFIELD
Cheltenham Unitarian

March 3rd

May we so pass through the things that are fleeting
As to be richer in the things that abide.
And may we so cherish the perishable beauties of life
That they may be imperishably present with us.[39]

JACOB TRAPP
1899–1992, Unitarian Universalist minister

March 4th*

We as Unitarians do not think we have *the* truth. At best,
we have *a* truth. In matters of faith, Unitarians do not
insist that only they are right … For us, something is
scripture because it is true, rather than being true because
it is in scripture … Are Unitarians Christians? How
narrowly do you want to define that term? If a Christian
is someone who agrees only with everything that one

* Faustus Socinus, Italian theologian who denied the divinity of Christ
and the doctrines of original sin and the atonement, died on this day
in 1604.

particular Church has laid down as universally applicable doctrine, then we aren't – and we don't want to be. We are glad to be heretics – people who choose for themselves.[40]

> DAVID USHER
> *Unitarian minister*

March 5th

Be with us, O God, when we think of the wrongs we have done to other people; lest, hating ourselves for our evil-doing, we turn our hatred outward on to them. Help us to forgive ourselves, acknowledging that we are no better than we are; and then help us to believe that we can be better.[41]

> A. POWELL DAVIES
> *1902–1957, Unitarian minister*

March 6th

Have regular hours for work and play; make each day both useful and pleasant, and prove that you understand the worth of time by employing it well. Then youth will be delightful, old age will bring few regrets, and life will become a beautiful success.[42]

> LOUISA MAY ALCOTT
> *Unitarian writer – author of* Little Women *– died on this day in 1888*

March 7th

In the end, only three things matter: how much you loved, how gently you lived, and how gracefully you let go of things not meant for you.

Attributed to THE BUDDHA

March 8th

International Women's Day

May it please your honor, I shall never pay a dollar of your unjust penalty.* All the stock in trade I possess is a $10,000 debt, incurred by publishing my paper – *The Revolution* – four years ago, the sole object of which was to educate all women to do precisely as I have done: rebel against your man-made, unjust, unconstitutional forms of law, that tax, fine, imprison and hang women, while they deny them the right of representation in the government; and I shall work on with might and main to pay every dollar of that honest debt, but not a penny shall go to this unjust claim. And I shall earnestly and persistently continue to urge all women to the practical recognition of the old revolutionary maxim, that "Resistance to tyranny is obedience to God".[43]

SUSAN B. ANTHONY
1820–1906, Unitarian and Quaker feminist and social reformer

---

* A fine of $100, imposed for "illegal voting" in 1872.

March 9th

I began to inquire what things were most common:
Air, Light, Heaven and Earth, Water, the Sun, Trees,
Men and Women, Cities, Temples, etc. These I found
common and obvious to all. Rubies, Pearls, Diamonds,
Gold and Silver; these I found scarce and to the most
denied. Then began I to consider and compare the value
of them, which I measured by their serviceableness, and
by the excellencies which would be found in them, should
they be taken away. And, in conclusion, I saw clearly that
there was a real valuableness in all the common things;
in the scarce, a feigned.[44]

THOMAS TRAHERNE

1636?–1674, mystic, theologian, metaphysical poet

March 10th

May we seek, acknowledge, and accept the truth about
the way things are. May we act at all times with kindliness
and friendliness: on the buses, in the shops, at our
workplace, and in our homes. And may our mindfulness
and kindliness flow directly from our hearts towards
all sentient beings in our world.

PEGGY MORGAN

Retired lecturer in the Study of Religion, University of Oxford

March 11th

In his death, James Reeb says something to each of us, black and white alike. He says that we must substitute courage for caution, says to us that we must be concerned not merely about who murdered him, but about the system, the way of life, the philosophy that produced the murder. His death says to us that we must work passionately, unrelentingly, to make the American dream a reality, so he did not die in vain.

DR MARTIN LUTHER KING JR.

Words spoken at the funeral of James Reeb, a Unitarian Universalist minister murdered during civil-rights protests in Selma, Alabama, on this day in 1965

March 12th

Friendship and domestic happiness are continually praised; yet how little is there of either in the world, because it requires more cultivation of mind to keep awake affection, even in our own hearts, than the common run of people suppose.[45]

MARY WOLLSTONECRAFT

Unitarian feminist, philosopher, and writer, 1759–1797

March 13th

Respect a parliamentary king, and chearfully pay
all parliamentary taxes; but have nothing to do with
a parliamentary religion, or a parliamentary God.
Religious rights, and religious liberty, are things of
inestimable value.[46]

JOSEPH PRIESTLEY
Unitarian minister, scientist, discoverer of oxygen,
liberal political philosopher, born on this day in 1733

March 14th

One of the most important things Amnesty International
did for me was to keep writing letters. Remember that
all totalitarian regimes have to make themselves appear
civilised. To do this they erect a huge bureaucracy.
A society of bureaucrats cannot throw away one piece
of paper without producing three other pieces. The worth
of a prisoner comes to be valued by the accumulated
documents – the number of letters in some cases.

IRINA RATUSHINSKAYA
1954–2017, Russian poet imprisoned by the KGB
for writing 'seditious' poetry

March 15th

In the glorious company of thy Christs and Buddhas,
in the concern for others of thy bodhisattvas and saints,
in the Good Samaritans of all ages who bring help
   and healing,
in the compassion of all who are brothers to their
   brothers,
we would bless and adore thee as goodness.[47]

JACOB TRAPP
1899–1992, Unitarian Universalist minister

March 16th

I have learned from long experience that there is nothing
that is not marvellous, and that the saying of Aristotle
is true: that in every natural phenomenon there is
something wonderful – nay, in truth, many wonders.
We are born and placed among wonders and surrounded
by them, so that to whatever object the eye first turns, the
same is full of wonders, if only we examine it for a while.

JOHN DE DUNDAS
14th-century philosopher

March 17th

We remember in thy sight all who are dear to us.
If we see them every day, let our feelings not be
    dulled by custom;
let us always be alive to the joys of true companionship.
If they are far from us, may they be helped and
strengthened by our unfailing affection,
and wherever they go, let them never lose the sense
    of thy love,
that protects and sustains the souls of all that truly
    seek thee.[48]

VERONA CONWAY
1910–1986, Unitarian minister at Lancaster 1963–1973

March 18th ★

Heresy simply means 'choice'. It came to mean 'thought crime', implying it was blasphemy to presume to choose your own belief instead of swallowing what the bishops spoonfed you.

ROBERT MCNAIR PRICE
American theologian and writer

★ On this day in 1612, Bartholomew Legate, anti-Trinitarian heretic, was burned at the stake in London for refusing to recant.

March 19th

Let there be peace in the Heavens; peace in the
Atmosphere; peace on Earth. Let the waters be cooling,
the herbs healing, and the plants enhancing Life. Let
there be peace and harmony between all beings in the
Universe. With perfection in knowledge, let peace pervade
everywhere. May this peace be throughout the World.
May there be peace among those around me, and may
there be peace within me as well.[49]

A HINDU PRAYER

March 20th

As surely as we belong to the universe, we belong
together. We join here to transcend the isolated self,
to reconnect, to know ourselves to be at home, here
on earth, under the stars, linked with each other.[50]

MARGARET KEIP
Unitarian Universalist minister

March 21st

"I can never remember people's names", says a friend of
mine. The reason he can never remember them is because
he never learned them in the first place. When the name
was announced to him, he was too busy thinking about
the impression he was making on this new person that he
never even momentarily paid any attention to the name.

How guilty are we all of this and similar inadvertence?
"To be awake is to be alive", writes Thoreau in *Walden*.
"I have never yet met a man who was quite awake.
How could I have looked him in the face?"[51]

BILL DARLISON
Unitarian minister, retired

March 22nd

This we know: the Earth does not not belong to us:
    we belong to the Earth.
This we know: all things are connected, like the blood
    which unites one family.
Whatever befalls the Earth befalls the sons and daughters
    of the Earth.
We did not weave the web of life: we are merely a
    strand in it.

Attributed to A NATIVE AMERICAN CHIEF

March 23rd

If we address the subject of our own death openly and
honestly, with calm acceptance (whatever our thoughts on
an after-life), and if we make whatever prior arrangements
we can, then we can move on. We can get on with the
really serious and important business of *life:* of loving
those around us, of speaking out for the things that we
believe in, of opposing injustice and intolerance, of being
active in the causes that we hold dear. This life that we

have here and now can be amazing, full of wonders.
If we allow it to be. This life can be full of love, full of
challenges, full of hopes, full of aspirations, full of beauty
– right up to its end. Let us all resolve that, whatever
befalls us, we will live our lives to the full.[52]

STEVE HODGES
Oxford Unitarian

March 24th

Anyone who proposes to do good must not expect
people to roll stones out of his way, but must accept
his lot calmly if they even roll a few more upon it. A
strength which becomes clearer and stronger through its
experience of such obstacles is the only strength that can
conquer them. Resistance is only a waste of strength. ...
Not one of us knows what effect his life produces, and
what he gives to others; that is hidden from us and must
remain so, though we are often allowed to see some little
fraction of it, so that we may not lose courage.[53]

ALBERT SCHWEITZER
*1875–1965, member of the Unitarian Universalist Church of the
Larger Fellowship, philosopher, musician, and doctor*

March 25th

It may well be that some composers do not believe in
God. All of them, however, believe in Bach.

BÉLA BARTØK
Hungarian composer and Unitarian, born on this day in 1881

March 26th

Remind us, God, that all people are deserving of your
love, and that we can be the agents of it. Help us
to respect the dignity of the old, and may we realise
our duty to bring them the fellowship that we ask for
ourselves. Remind us, then, of those who are alone,
but remind us also that they are alone because we
have not gone to them.[54]

CLIFF REED
Unitarian minister, retired

March 27th

I searched but I could not find Thee.
I called thee aloud standing on the minaret.
I rang the temple bell
with the rising and setting of the Sun.
I bathed in the Ganges in vain.
I came back from Kaaba disappointed.
I looked for thee on the earth.
I searched for thee in the heavens, my Beloved.
And at last, I have found thee,
hidden as a pearl in the shell of my Heart.

PIR INAYAT KHAN
1916–2004, Sufi teacher and President of the Sufi Order International

March 28th

The goal of all religion is not to prepare us to enter the next life; it is a call to live now, to love now, to be now – and in that way to taste what it means to be part of a life that is eternal, a love that is barrier-free, and the being of a fully self-conscious humanity. That is the doorway into a universal consciousness that is part of what the word 'God' now means to me. This then becomes my pathway into the meaning of life that is eternal. It starts when we step beyond our hiding place in religion into thinking, and finally into being. It involves stepping beyond boundaries into wholeness, beyond a limited consciousness into a universal consciousness, beyond a God who is other into a God who is all.[55]

JOHN SHELBY SPONG
Former Episcopal Bishop of Newark, New Jersey

March 29th

I thank You God for knowing me better than I know
    myself,
and for letting me know myself better than others
    know me.
Make me, I ask You then, better than they suppose,
and forgive me for what they do not know.

ABU BAKR
father-in-law of the Prophet Muhammad

March 30th

Source of all being, mysterious presence: we give thanks
for all artists in whatever media they work, for helping
us to see something not present, for bridging the gaps
in reality, and for leading us to new ways of thinking.
… Open our eyes and ears to all that is around us – the
majestic and the mundane, that we might appreciate
both the awesome and the everyday. … We are daily
confronted by examples of failure in imagination:
in personal relationships, in political life, in industry.
Help us to see beyond the detail and the conflict to the
imaginative solution.[56]

DAVID DAWSON
Musician, writer, and member of the Bradford Unitarian congregation

March 31st

We need to view the cross as a symbol of the problem
(sin), rather than the solution (salvation). The cross
did not take away sin. The cross *is* sin. … Did Jesus die
for my sins? Perhaps that is true in some metaphorical
sense, but more importantly I must say that people today,
in the developing world, and in the streets of our cities,
are dying for my sins – or rather because of my sins,
because of the interdependent web of collective sin
that we live in: economic and political systems in which
we all participate.[57]

STEPHEN LINGWOOD
Unitarian minister, Cardiff

APRIL

April 1st

What soap is to the body, laughter is to the soul.

YIDDISH PROVERB

DEAR WASHERS-UP: PLEASE RINSE THE TEAPOTS
AND THEN STAND UPSIDE DOWN IN THE SINK
A notice in the kitchen of Unitarian New Meeting, Birmingham

April 2nd

Finish every day and be done with it. You have done what
you could. Some blunders and absurdities no doubt crept
in; forget them as soon as you can. Tomorrow is a new
day; begin it well and serenely and with too high a spirit
to be cumbered with your old nonsense. This day is too
dear to waste a moment on the yesterdays.

RALPH WALDO EMERSON
*1803–1882, Unitarian minister, essayist, and philosopher,
Boston, Massachusetts*

April 3rd

Let there be light:

The light of joy, the light of happiness, and the light
    of contentment.

May it illuminate our paths and fill our lives with peace.

And let there be dark.

For it is from our dark places that we are brought forward,

Tried and tested, and impelled towards growth.

It is in these places that we realise compassion and
    learn to love.[58]

ANDREW PAKULA
Minister of New Unity Unitarian Church, London

April 4th

I have learned to live each day as it comes, and not to
borrow trouble by dreading tomorrow.

DOROTHEA DIX
Unitarian social reformer, 1802–1887, born on this day

April 5th

What religious beliefs are we holding on to that are
useless to us? Do our experiences and our beliefs hang
together, or are we lazily still accepting other people's
views which we have not been quite brave enough to
drop? When are we going to explore beliefs and live
more bravely? When are we going to think for ouselves?

We should not be weighed down by the clutter of the past, but review it, dismiss as much of it as we feel able, and march into the future with a lightness of heart. Life moves on, and so do we. Let us start today.[59]

PENNY JOHNSON
Unitarian minister, retired

April 6th

A man is really ethical only when he obeys the constraint laid on him to help all life which he is able to succour, and when he goes out of his way to avoid injuring anything living. He does not ask how far this or that life deserves sympathy as valuable in itself, nor how far it is capable of feeling. To him, life as such is sacred. He shatters no ice crystal that sparkles in the sun, tears no leaf from its tree, breaks off no flower, and is careful not to crush any insect as he walks.[60]

ALBERT SCHWEITZER
1875–1965, philosopher, musician, and doctor; member of the Unitarian Universalist Church of the Larger Fellowship

April 7th

I am a living member of the great family of all souls and cannot improve or suffer myself without diffusing good or evil around me through an ever-enlarging sphere. I belong to this family. I am bound to it by vital bonds.

I am always exerting influence on it. I can hardly perform an act that is confined in its consequences to myself. Others are affected by what I am and say and do, so a single act of mine may spread and spread in widening circles, through a nation or humanity.[61]

WILLIAM ELLERY CHANNING
1780–1842, Unitarian minister and theologian,
England and America, born on this day

April 8th

Thank you to the woman on the Underground train. Surrounded by tight, hard faces, her hair wafting in the sooty breeze, she stood with her eyes defencelessly closed, and a look of calm delight on her face. She was obviously there, but clearly somewhere else as well – and not minding who saw it and knew it. The rattle-bang of the carriage became a softer and lighter place for the seeing. … Is our spiritual balance for our own benefit, or is it for the sake of leaking peacefulness into our surroundings, of shedding gentleness into our relationships, of witnessing depths in a shallow world?[62]

MICHAEL DADSON
Unitarian minister, retired

April 9th

No house should ever be on a hill or on anything. It should be *of* the hill. Belonging to it. Hill and house should live together, each the happier for the other.

Nature is my manifestation of God. I go to nature every day for inspiration in the day's work. I follow in building the principles which nature has used in its domain.

FRANK LLOYD WRIGHT
Unitarian architect and philosopher, died on this day in 1959

April 10th

The least pain in our little finger gives us more concern and uneasiness than the destruction of millions of our fellow-beings.[63]

WILLIAM HAZLITT
1778–1830, Unitarian essayist and critic, born on this day

April 11th

I want to stand as close to the edge as I can without going over. Out on the edge you see all the kinds of things you can't see from the center.

KURT VONNEGUT
Unitarian Universalist author – of Slaughterhouse Five, *and other radical works – died on this day in 2007*

April 12th

I have an almost complete disregard of precedent, and a faith in the possibility of something better. It irritates me to be told how things have always been done. I defy the tyranny of precedence. I go for anything new that might improve the past.[64]

CLARA BARTON
Universalist founder of the American Red Cross,
died on this day in 1922

April 13th

We hold these truths to be self-evident: that all men are created equal; that they are endowed by their Creator with certain unalienable rights; that among these are life, liberty, and the pursuit of happiness.[65]

THOMAS JEFFERSON
Unitarian President of the United States, born on this day in 1743

April 14th

For I will consider my Cat Jeoffry.
For he is the servant of the Living God, duly and daily
  serving him. ...
For he keeps the Lord's watch in the night against the
  adversary.
For he counteracts the powers of darkness by his
  electrical skin and glaring eyes.

For in his morning orisons he loves the sun and the sun
  loves him. …
For he purrs in thankfulness when God tells him he's
  a good Cat.
For he is an instrument for the children to learn
  benevolence upon.
For every house is incomplete without him, and a
  blessing is lacking in the spirit.[66]

CHRISTOPHER SMART
English poet, 1722–1751

April 15th

Jewish prayer includes a daily blessing for opening the eyes
of the blind. My dog must be God's agent, because he
shows me numerous wonders that I would otherwise have
missed. Wearing down my resistance with a mournful
stare, he takes me out at midnight. We watch the clouds
flee past the moon and a hedgehog run on tiny legs for
the long grass. … Dogs rarely interrupt, never say the
wrong thing, and have an unimpeachable record on
confidentiality. … Dogs expand our capacity for love. They
love unconditionally. … They do not harbour resentments
when you get back home after going out without them:
they pardon you with all their heart, all their tail, and all
their eager nose.[67]

JONATHAN WITTENBURG
Senior Rabbi for Masorti Judaism

April 16th

We must develop and maintain the capacity to forgive. He who is devoid of the power to forgive is devoid of the power to love. There is some good in the worst of us and some evil in the best of us. When we discover this, we are less prone to hate our enemies.[68]

MARTIN LUTHER KING, JR.
1929–1968, civil-rights leader

April 17th

This is the time when the earth is renewing herself peacefully, marvellously, victoriously. No power on earth may push back this triumphant tide of life. … We are grateful that we ourselves are part of this great and glorious ordering. … All unseen, the goodness of the air blesses every cell and fibre of our bodies, while silently our blood circulates through our veins, food strengthens us, and water, so humble and precious and clean, daily bestows its vital blessings. We are part of the ceaseless web of life, part of the harmony in the eternal song of praise; we resolve not to break, through stupidity, carelessness, or greed, the lovely and delicate strains of life's web; not to bring discord and ugliness into the music of life.[69]

FRANK WALKER
Unitarian minister, retired

April 18th

Infinite Spirit of Life … may we cherish friendship as one of thy most precious gifts. May we not let awareness of another's talents discourage us, or sully our relationship, but may we realize that, whatever we can do, great or small, the efforts of all of us are needed to do thy work in this world.

NORBERT ČAPEK
Czech Unitarian minister, died at Dachau in 1942

April 19th ★

We stand on the shoulders of giants – of the heretics and dissenters who gave selflessly for the principles we still hold dear.

DEREK MCAULEY
Former Chief Officer, General Assembly of Unitarian and Free Christian Churches

April 20th

We demand facts, not stories, we crave the security of certainty, and are afraid of mystery. We have denied ourselves our dreams, we have starved ourselves of stories, and we wonder why we are unhappy. Yet happiness

★ Katherine Vogel, Unitarian martyr, died at the stake on this day in 1539 in Poland.

and joy are within our reach. Like God, they are never more than a heartbeat away. Our happiness and joy, like God, are hidden within our sorrows.[70]

TOM MCCREADY
Unitarian minister, Hull

April 21st

We exchange a God with a 'throne' and a 'foot-stool', a 'right-hand seat' and a left, for the Living Presence of a Universal Mind, looking into our eyes in all that is beautiful, and communing with us in all that is right.[71]

JAMES MARTINEAU
Unitarian theologian and philosopher, born on this day in 1805; died 1901

April 22nd
Earth Day

Love all of God's creation, both the whole and every grain of sand in it. Love every leaf, every ray of light. Love the animals, love the plants, love every kind of thing. If you love each fragment, then everywhere God's mystery will reveal itself to you. Once you perceive it, you will begin to understand it ever more deeply with each passing day. And finally you will be able to love the whole world with an all-embracing universal love.[72]

FYODOR DOSTOYEVSKY
1821–1881

April 23rd

O God to whom we come so often with needs to be satisfied, help us to come sometimes in gratitude for what we already have. For the rest and renewal of the nighttime and the freshness of morning ... for the love of friends, and kindness and compassion when we need them; for the joy of human fellowship, and work to do; for all the ventures and endeavors in which we depend upon each other ... for the values that we take for granted, and for so much goodness in our common daily life.[73]

A. POWELL DAVIES
1902–1957, Unitarian minister

April 24th

Simply to be, and to let things be as they speak wordlessly from the mystery of what they are; simply to say a silent yes to the hillside flowers, to the trees we walk under; to pass from one person to another a morsel of bread, an answering yes: this is the simplest, the quietest, of sacraments.

JACOB TRAPP
1899–1992, Unitarian Universalist minister

April 25th

Help us to love the world aright. Help us to add to its beauty, not just to its static loveliness, but to its onward-going life and grace. ... Help us to love our neighbour aright, and, if that is what is needed, to love ourselves aright. ... Make us, we pray, those who, imperfect beings in an imperfect world, still love that which is perfect, and strive to live accordingly.[74]

HARRY LISMER SHORT
1906–1975, Unitarian Principal of Manchester College Oxford

April 26th

If you want to be spiritually healthy, you need to practise your spirituality. You can choose what your practice will be. But having chosen it, you have to do it. For some, it might be regular church-going, even on those Sunday mornings when they really would prefer to lie in bed or go to the garden centre. For others, it might be meditation, chanting, yoga, t'ai chi – you name it. Whatever it is, the important thing is that you do it.[75]

DAVID USHER
Unitarian minister

April 27th

In the woods a man casts off his years, as the snake his skin, and at whatever period of life he is always a child. … There I feel that nothing can befall me in life – no disgrace, no calamity – which nature cannot repair. Standing on the bare ground – my head bathed by the blithe air, and uplifted into infinite space – all mean egotism vanishes. I become a transparent eyeball; I am nothing; I see all; the currents of the Universal Being circulate through me; I am part or particle of God.[76]

RALPH WALDO EMERSON
*1803–1882, Unitarian minister, essayist, and philosopher,
Boston, Massachusetts; died on this day*

April 28th

We are being overwhelmed by a surging culture of cupidity. We are being encouraged to pursue our wants without any regard for moral balance, and in envy of those who have already acquired the things that we want. They, of course, now want something bigger and better. The culture of cupidity has permeated the topmost layer of our society. As Herbert Butterfield once wrote: *'A civilisation may be wrecked without any spectacular crimes, but by constant petty breaches of faith and minor complicities on the part of those generally considered very nice people'.*[77]

JOHN TOYE
Cambridge Unitarian

April 29th

Look to this day, for it is life – the very life of life.
In its brief course lie all the realities and truths
    of existence,
the joy of growth, the splendour of action, the
    glory of power.
For yesterday is but a memory, and tomorrow is
    only a vision.
But today well lived makes every yesterday a
    memory of happiness,
and every tomorrow a vision of hope.
Look well, therefore, to this day…

SANSKRIT POEM, ASCRIBED TO KALIDASA
Hindu poet of the third century CE

April 30th

There is no God in the sky. God is in the heart that loves
the sky's blueness.

A. POWELL DAVIES
1902–1957, Unitarian minister, Washington, DC

MAY

May 1st
International Workers' Day

Before we leave our home each day, we are beholden to workers in far countries. The soaps and scents that we use to clean and freshen ourselves start in minerals from mines and wells in distant lands. Our coffee, tea, fruit juice, and cornflakes are grown for us by people we have not met. Our lives coincide only in the moment when we take what they have given. What we eat or drink makes little difference to us; yet we know that our choice can make a vast difference to those who supply our food. On this day we pray that all over the world, in industry, commerce, and trade, women and men may labour in safety; that owners, proprietors, and managers will honour their workers and the sacred memory of those who have been harmed and even killed by their job.[78]

JEFFREY BOWES
Unitarian minister, retired

May 2nd

I look only to the good qualities of men. Not being faultless myself, I won't presume to probe into the faults of others.

MAHATMA GANDHI
1869–1948, Indian independence leader

May 3rd

I still call myself a communist, because communism is no more what Russia made of it than Christianity is what the churches make of it.[79]

PETE SEEGER
1919–2014, Unitarian Universalist folk singer and social activist,
born on this day

May 4th

Time is relative to the speed of light; it is not a universal constant, as Albert Einstein said. Looking at the sun, we see it where it was about 8 minutes ago. There are visible stars in the night sky which no longer exist. ... Time is something with meaning only in relation to our finite temporal existence, whereas Ultimate Reality, or Being Itself (what we refer to as God) is beyond time, and when we are in union with God, so are we. 'With the Lord one day is as a thousand years, and a thousand years as one day' (2 Peter 3 v. 8). In other words, there is no time with God – there is only the eternal NOW. Eternal does not mean 'everlasting' – an endless stretch of time – it is beyond time. God is not thousands of millions of years old. God is NOW. [80]

DAVID MONK
Unitarian minister, leader of the Meditation Fellowship, died 2011

May 5th

Your children are not your children. They are the sons and daughters of life's longing for itself. They come through you, but not from you. And though they are with you, they belong not to you. You may give them your love but not your thoughts. You may house their bodies, but not their souls. For their souls dwell in the house of tomorrow, which you cannot visit, not even in your dreams. You may strive to be like them, but seek not to make them like you. [81]

KAHLIL GIBRAN
1883–1931, Lebanese-American writer and artist

May 6th

What lies behind us and what lies ahead of us are tiny matters compared with what lives within us. And when we bring what is within out into the world, miracles happen.

HENRY DAVID THOREAU
1817–1862, Transcendentalist writer and thinker,
raised Unitarian in Massachusetts, died on this day

May 7th

Afoot and light-hearted I take to the open road,
Healthy, free, the world before me,
The long brown path before me leading wherever
    I choose.

Henceforth I ask not good-fortune, I myself am
    good-fortune,
Henceforth I whimper no more, postpone no more,
    need nothing,
Done with indoor complaints, libraries, querulous
    criticisms,
Strong and content I travel the open road.[82]

WALT WHITMAN
1819–1892, American poet and essayist

May 8th

We pray for a keener delight in the world around us.
Delight in its loveliness, its colours, scents and sounds.
Delight in the fascinating structure of nature and of the
human form. Delight in the saga of the past, in story, song
and movement, in art and science, and in good work well
done. Delight in the present moment in all its richness.

FRANK WALKER
Unitarian minister, retired

May 9th

Men have banned divinity from their midst, they have
relegated it inside a sanctuary. The walls of a temple are
the limits of its view; beyond these walls it does not exist.
You must destroy these barriers that limit your horizon;
set God free [*élargissez Dieu*]; see Him everywhere, where
he actually is, or otherwise say that he does not exist.[83]

DENIS DIDEROT
1713–1784, French philosopher

May 10th

It takes years to marry completely two hearts, even of the
most loving and well assorted. A happy wedlock is a long
falling in love. Young persons think love belongs only to
the brown-haired and crimson-cheeked. So it does for its
beginning. But the golden marriage is a part of love which
the bridal day knows nothing of. …

THEODORE PARKER
Unitarian minister and Transcendentalist in Boston, Massachusetts,
died on this day in 1860

May 11th

God is not so much a being
as the word we use when confronted
with the totality of all being,
the unimaginable ultimacy of the universe,
and the mystery of love
at work in the human heart.[84]

CLIFF REED
Unitarian minister, retired

May 12th

It is often thought that medicine is the curative process.
It is no such thing; medicine is the surgery of functions,
as surgery proper is that of limbs and organs. Neither can
do anything but remove obstructions; neither can cure;
nature alone cures. Surgery removes the bullet out of
the limb, which is an obstruction to cure, but nature
heals the wound. So it is with medicine; the function
of an organ becomes obstructed; medicine assists nature
to remove the obstruction, but does nothing more.
And what nursing has to do in either case is to put the
patient in the best condition for nature to act upon him.[85]

FLORENCE NIGHTINGALE
1820–1910, raised as a Unitarian; social reformer,
statistician, founder of modern nursing; born on this day

May 13th

I belong to the Great Church which holds the world
within its starlit aisles; that claims the great and good of
every race and clime; that finds with joy the grain of gold
in every creed, and floods with light and love the germs
of good in every soul.[86]

ROBERT INGERSOLL

1833–1899, American political leader, orator, Unitarian agnostic

May 14th

A hero is no braver than an ordinary man, but he is braver
five minutes longer.

RALPH WALDO EMERSON

1803–1882, Unitarian minister, essayist, and philosopher,
Boston, Massachusetts

May 15th

Nobody joins a church in order to join a committee.
Nobody in their right mind, anyway. However, serving
on a committee, or helping to make the tea, or
volunteering to arrange the flowers, or visiting a sick
person house-bound or in hospital, all of these things
are done in service to the community and the individuals
in that community, and in that service one discovers the
reward of contributing to the common good. They are
not done for immediate personal gain. But in doing those

things, one discovers personal gain. A healthy personal
spirituality is discovered as part of a larger community.[87]

DAVID USHER
Unitarian minister

May 16th

Make the most of your regrets; never smother your sorrow,
but tend and cherish it till it comes to have a separate and
integral interest. To regret deeply is to live afresh.

HENRY DAVID THOREAU
1817–1862, Transcendentalist writer and thinker,
raised Unitarian in Massachusetts

May 17th

Let us be aware of the source of being common to us
all, and to all living things. Invoking the presence of the
Great Compassion, let us fill our hearts with our own
compassion – towards ourselves and towards all living
beings. Let us pray that all living beings realise that they
are brothers and sisters, all nourished from the same
source of life. Let us commit ourselves to live in a way
which will not deprive other living beings of the chance
to live. Let us pray for the establishment of peace in
our hearts and on earth.

BUDDHIST PRAYER

May 18th

You never enjoy the world aright till the sea itself
floweth in your veins, till you are clothed with the
heavens, and crowned with the stars, and perceive
yourself to be the sole heir of the whole world, and
more than so, because men are in it who are every one
sole heirs as well as you. Till you can sing and rejoice
and delight in God, as misers do in gold, and kings
in sceptres, you never enjoy the world.[88]

THOMAS TRAHERNE
1636–1674, English poet and theologian

May 19th

There is power in love. Don't under-estimate it.
Don't over-sentimentalise it. ... The source of love is
God. ... God is love. ... Love God. Love your neighbours.
And while you're at it, love yourself. ... When love is the
way, we will let justice roll down like a mighty river and
righteousness like an ever-flowing stream. ... Poverty will
become history. ... The earth will become a sanctuary.
... We will lay down our swords and shields down by the
riverside. When love is the way, there's plenty good room
for all of God's children.[89]

MICHAEL CURRY
*Episcopalian Bishop, preaching at a royal wedding in
St George's Chapel, Windsor, on this day in 2018*

May 20th

At Judgement Day everyone will have to give an account of every good thing which he might have enjoyed but did not enjoy.[90]

JEWISH SCRIPTURE: KIDDUSH 66D

May 21st

The years of all of us are short, our lives precarious. Our days and nights go hurrying on, and there is scarcely time to do the little that we might. Yet we find time for bitterness, for petty treason and evasion. What can we do to stretch our hearts enough to lose their littleness? Here we are – all of us upon this planet – bound together in a common destiny, living our lives between the briefness of the daylight and the dark. Kindred in this, each lighted by the same precarious, flickering flame of life, how does it happen that we are not kindred in all things else? How strange and foolish are these walls of separation that divide us![91]

A. POWELL DAVIES
1902–1957, Unitarian minister, Washington, DC

May 22nd

I am far too busy to pray for anything less than two hours a day.

BISHOP DESMOND TUTU
Former Archbishop of Cape Town

May 23rd

It is astonishing what force, purity, and wisdom it requires for a human being to keep clear of falsehoods.

MARGARET FULLER
1810–1850. Unitarian journalist and feminist, born on this day

May 24th

Try to start every meeting with another person by being as fully present as possible, and attending to what the other has to communicate to you, both verbally and non-verbally. I try to enter every meeting with an open heart, open mind, and open will, open to what emerges. This involves pausing before I enter, noticing my emotions and fears, my thoughts and assumptions, as well as my preconceptions – and letting them go, so that I am ready to be present to what might happen and what might surprise me.[92]

PETER HAWKINS
Unitarian, management consultant, and author

May 25th

The task of religion is to comfort the afflicted, and to afflict the comfortable.

RALPH WALDO EMERSON
*1803–1882, Unitarian minister, essayist,
and philosopher, born on this day*

May 26th

Vices to Virtues

O God please grant me
enough anger to tackle wrongdoing
enough pride in family, friends and community
enough deceit to pay attention to the tender
    feelings of others
enough envy to admire people's good deeds
enough avarice to hoard the world's resources
enough fear to avoid dangerous living
enough gluttony to savour every flavour
enough lust to live life to the full
enough sloth to be in and down, here and now.[93]

JOSEPHINE SECCOMBE
Oxford Unitarian

May 27th

Faith in an infinitely perfect God is our theology.
The Universe is our divine revelation. The manifestations
of nature and the devotional literature of all times
and peoples are our Bible. The goodness incarnated in
humanity is our Christ. Every guide and helper is our
Saviour. Increasing personal holiness is our salvation.
The normal wonders of nature are our miracles. Love
of God and love of man are our only sacraments.

FRANCIS WILLIAM NEWMAN
Unitarian scholar, 1805–1897

May 28th

One of our most important tasks as Unitarians is to
convince others that there is nothing to fear in difference;
that difference, in fact, is one of the healthiest and most
invigorating of human characteristics, without which life
would become meaningless. Here lies the power of the
liberal way: not in making the whole world Unitarian,
but in helping ourselves and others to see some of the
possibilities inherent in viewpoints other than one's
own; in encouraging the free interchange of ideas;
in welcoming fresh approaches to the problems of life;
in urging the fullest, most vigorous use of critical
self-examination.[94]

ADLAI STEVENSON
1900–1965, Unitarian politician, diplomat and 'universal citizen'

May 29th

Happiness is like a butterfly which, when pursued, is always beyond our grasp. But if you will sit down quietly, it may alight upon you.

NATHANIEL HAWTHORNE
American novelist, 1804–1864

May 30th

Do not attach yourself to any particular creed so exclusively that you disbelieve all the rest; otherwise you will lose much good; nay, you will fail to recognise the real truth of the matter. God, the omnipresent and omnipotent, is not limited by any one creed, for, he says, "Wheresoever ye turn, there is the face of Allah." … Everyone praises what he believes; his god is his own creature, and in praising it he praises himself. Consequently he criticises the beliefs of others, which he would not do if he were just; but his dislike is based on ignorance.

MUID AD-DIN IBN AL-ARABI
Sufi philosopher, 1164–1240

May 31st

For me, worship is not a transitive verb. Worship does
not require an object in order to be grammatically correct.
In fact, quite the opposite. Worship with an object has
for me ceased to be worship in its pure and proper sense.
Worship is the act of reminding myself of values that the
world would otherwise make me forget. … I invite you
to consider what worship is for you. Is it a transitive verb?
Are you paying homage to a something or a someone?
Or is it intransitive? Are you placing yourself in the
company of the holy, keeping your soul healthy and
aware and alive?[95]

DAVID USHER
Unitarian minister

JUNE

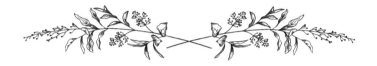

June 1st

Come into a space of quiet and peace. Close your eyes.
Sit straight. Breathe deeply ... Open your eyes and look
at your hands. They have been through a lot, those hands.
They have strengths, scars, and beauty. It is your hands
that do the work of love in the world. These hands may
hold another's ... type emails to politicians ... sign cards
of consolation or congratulation. These hands may
patiently teach ... quilt works of beauty, or write words
urging peace. These hands may bathe children ...
feed an old person ... nurse the sick ... work the earth
... organise communities. These hands clasp in prayer
... open in release ... grasp in solidarity ... clench in
righteous anger. These hands are God's hands, your
hands, our hands; a great mystery of flesh and intention,
a great potential of embodied love.[96]

ANONYMOUS UNITARIAN WRITER

June 2nd

God does not die on the day when we cease to believe
in a personal deity, but we die on the day when our
lives cease to be illuminated by a steady radiance,
renewed daily, of a wonder, the source of which is
beyond all reason.[97]

DAG HAMMARSKJÖLD
1905–1961, Unitarian; second Secretary General of the United Nations

June 3rd

The Taliban shot me. They shot my friends too.
They thought they would change my aims and stop
my ambitions, but nothing changed in my life except
this: weakness, fear, and hopelessness died. Strength,
power, and courage was born. I am the same Malala.
My dreams are the same. I am not against anyone,
nor am I here to speak in terms of personal revenge
against the Taliban or any other terrorist group. I'm
here to speak up for the right of education for every
child. I want education for the sons and daughters
of the Taliban and all terrorists and extremists.

MALALA YOUSAFZAI
addressing the United Nations General Assembly in 2013

June 4th

The book of all books is in your own heart, in which are written and engraven the deepest lessons of divine instruction; learn therefore to be deeply attentive to the presence of God in your hearts – the God who is always speaking, always instructing, always illuminating the heart that is attentive.[98]

WILLIAM LAW
Anglican priest and theologian, 1686–1761

June 5th

World Environment Day

When you defile the pleasant streams
And the wild bird's abiding place,
You massacre a million dreams
And cast your spittle in God's face.

JOHN DRINKWATER
English poet and dramatist, 1882–1937

June 6th

I look upon all men as my compatriots, and embrace a Pole as a Frenchman, making less account of the national than of the universal and common bond.

MICHEL DE MONTAIGNE
1533–1592, philosopher and essayist

June 7th

In the streets and society I am almost invariably cheap and dissipated, my life is unspeakably mean. But alone in the distant woods or field, in unpretending sprout-lands or pastures tracked by rabbits, even on a bleak and, to most, cheerless day like this, when a villager would be thinking of his inn, I come to myself, I once more feel myself grandly related, and that cold and solitude are friends of mine. I come home to my solitary woodland walk as the homesick go home. I thus dispose of the superfluous and see things as they are.[99]

HENRY DAVID THOREAU
1817–1862, Transcendentalist poet, philosopher, and naturalist,
raised as a Unitarian

June 8th

There are few prophets in the world; few sublimely beautiful women; few heroes. I can't afford to give all my love and reverence to such rarities: I want a great deal of those feelings for my every-day fellow-men, especially for the few in the foreground of the great multitude, whose faces I know, whose hands I touch, for whom I have to make way with kindly courtesy.[100]

GEORGE ELIOT (MARY ANN EVANS)
1819–1880; novelist; member of the Rosslyn Hill
Unitarian congregation, Hampstead

June 9th

Spirituality, in order to develop, needs time for contemplation, just as a young plant needs water. But busyness has become one of the great badges of pride in our consumer culture. 'Empty' time must be filled by getting, spending, and connecting. This emphasis on doing, rather than being, has created addictive patterns of behaviour across the population. Mobile phones are a case in point. Surveys increasingly show that people become anxious to the point of incapacity if they cannot access their phone. For the sake of our spiritual lives, we must strive to resist these pressures.[101]

JOHN NAISH
Unitarian journalist and author

June 10th

These roses under my window make no reference to
former roses or to better ones; they are what they are;
they exist with God today. There is no time to them.
There is simply the rose; it is perfect in every moment of
its existence. ... But we postpone or remember. We do not
live in the present, but with reverted eye lament the past,
or, heedless of the riches that surround us, stand on tiptoe
to foresee the future. We cannot be happy or strong until
we too live with nature in the present, above time.[102]

RALPH WALDO EMERSON
1803–1882, Unitarian minister, essayist, and philosopher,
Boston, Massachusetts

June 11th

Till your spirit filleth the whole world, and the stars
are your jewels; till you are as familiar with the ways of
God in all Ages as with your walk and table: till you are
intimately acquainted with that shady nothing out of
which the world was made: till you love men so as to
desire their happiness, with a thirst equal to the zeal of
your own: till you delight in God for being good to all:
you never enjoy the world.[103]

THOMAS TRAHERNE
c.1636–1674, English poet, priest, and theologian

June 12th

O our Mother the Earth, O our Father the Sky,
Your children are we, and with tired backs
We bring you the gifts you love.
Then weave us a garment of brightness;
May the warp be the white light of morning,
May the weft be the red light of evening,
May the fringes be the falling rain,
May the border be the standing rainbow.
Thus weave us a garment of brightness,
That we may walk fittingly where birds sing,
That we may walk fittingly where grass is green,
O our Mother the Earth, O our Father the Sky.

A PRAYER OF THE TEWA PEOPLE
a sub-group of Pueblo Native Americans

June 13th

Man has been endowed with reason, with the power
to create, so that he can add to what he's been given.
But up to now he hasn't been a creator, only a destroyer.
Forests keep disappearing, rivers dry up, wild lives become
extinct, the climate ruined and the land grows poorer
and uglier every day.[104]

ANTON CHEKHOV
1860–1904

June 14th

Anniversary of the Grenfell Tower fire in 2017

It was not 'the poor' who died in the Grenfell Tower fire:
it was our brothers and sisters.

BROTHER JOSEPH EMMANUEL
(Society of St Francis)
Guest preacher at an Oxford Unitarian service

We affirm a continuing hope –
That out of every tragedy
the spirit of individuals shall rise
to build a better world.[105]

LEONARD MASON
1912–1995, Unitarian minister in England and Canada

June 15th ★

At Runnymede, at Runnymede,
Your rights were won at Runnymede!
No freeman shall be fined or bound,
Or dispossessed of freehold ground,
Except by lawful judgement found
And passed upon him by his peers!
Forget not, after all these years,
The Charter signed at Runnymede.

RUDYARD KIPLING
1865–1936

★ The Magna Carta was signed by King John on this day in 1215.

June 16th

We shall pass through this world but once. If there is any good we can do, or any kindness we can show, to man, or woman, child or beast, let us do it now; let us not neglect or defer it; for we shall not pass this way again.[106]

HARRY LISMER SHORT
1906–1975, Unitarian Principal of Manchester College Oxford

June 17th

Nothing that lives is, or can be, rigidly perfect; part of it is decaying, part nascent. The foxglove blossom, a third part bud, a third part past, a third part in full bloom, is a type of the life of this world. And in all things that live there are certain irregularities and deficiencies which are not only signs of life, but sources of beauty. All admit irregularity as they imply change; and to banish imperfection is to destroy expression, to check exertion, to paralyse vitality.[107]

JOHN RUSKIN
1819–1900, art critic, artist, social thinker and philanthropist

June 18th

We have begged for peace around the world.
We have fought for peace around the world.
We have contributed funds to peace around the world.
We have given great speeches for peace around the world.
Yet we have failed to make peace with our husbands
    and wives,
Our children, and our neighbours.

It is not enough to proclaim peace to the end of the earth.
Unless a man can make peace with those nearest to him,
He has not found religion. May we find religion in our
    daily living.[108]

PHILIP LARSON
1919–1996, Unitarian Universalist

June 19th

I can do no other than be reverent before everything
    that is called life.
I can do no other than to have compassion for all that
    is called life.
That is the beginning and the foundation of all ethics.

ALBERT SCHWEITZER
*1875–1965, philosopher, musician, and doctor; member of the
Unitarian Universalist Church of the Larger Fellowship*

June 20th

The birds have dissolved into the sky,
And the last remaining clouds have faded away.
We sit together, the mountain and me,
Until only the mountain remains.

LI PO
701–762, Chinese poet of the Tang dynasty

June 21st

We humans think we are smart, but an orchid, for
example, knows how to produce noble, symmetrical
flowers, and a snail knows how to make a beautiful,
well-proportioned shell. Compared with their knowledge,
ours is not worth much at all. We should bow deeply
before the orchid and the snail and join our palms
reverently before the monarch butterfly and the magnolia
tree. The feeling of respect for all species will help
us recognise the noblest nature in ourselves.

THE VENERABLE THICH NHAT HANH
1926–, Vietnamese Buddhist monk and teacher

June 22nd

This being human is a guest house. Every morning
is a new arrival. A joy, a depression, a meanness, some
momentary awareness comes as an unexpected visitor …
Welcome and entertain them all. Treat each guest
honorably. The dark thought, the shame, the malice,
meet them at the door laughing, and invite them in.
Be grateful for whoever comes, because each has been
sent as a guide from beyond.

JALAL UL-DIN RUMI
1207–1273, poet, scholar, theologian, Sufi mystic

June 23rd

Find a quiet place to sit comfortably. Hold an acorn or
a nut in your hand, look at it for a long time then touch
it gently. Close your eyes, and allow the image of it to
remain clear in your mind. After a few moments, allow
yourself to imagine the slow emerging of the tree into
which it can grow. Appreciate the wonder of the growth
of something so massive emerging from something so
tiny. Stay with the feeling of wonder, and let the images
fade away. Remain sitting quietly. Be still.[109]

JANE BARTON
Unitarian minister, retired

June 24th
Midsummer's Day

Such a day it was as – looking back –
imbues a whole Summer's memories with warmth
and places a gold overlay on all grey.
Larks lifted at my feet
and climbed, cascading sound, to vanishing point
in faded denim skies.
Foals like glossy chestnuts newly split
lay fallen in their mothers' shadows
and lizards flickered the furze through.

At length the river valley wound below for respite,
where moorland cattle, unkempt in dark brown habits,
bowed their heads around a granite cross
and grazed by beneficial waters.
Nor moved when I approached, but by their gaze
defied me not to join their worship there.[110]

RICHARD LOVIS
Unitarian writer and lay leader; deceased

June 25th

The most important relationship we can all have is the one you have with yourself, the most important journey you can take is one of self-discovery. To know yourself, you must spend time with yourself, you must not be afraid to be alone. Knowing yourself is the beginning of all wisdom.

ARISTOTLE
384–322 BCE

*June 26th**

Let us teach that the honour of a nation consists not in the forced submission of other states, but in equal laws and free institutions, in cultivated fields and prosperous cities; in the development of intellectual and moral power … magnanimity and justice, the virtues and blessings of peace. … We should honour nations for their free institutions, wise laws, promotion of humane education, benevolence and justice.

WILLIAM ELLERY CHANNING
1780–1842, Unitarian minister and theologian, England and America

* The Charter of the United Nations was signed on this day in 1945.

June 27th

I want to say to those who are trying to learn to speak and those who are teaching them: Be of good cheer. Do not think of to-day's failures, but of the success that may come to-morrow. You have set yourselves a difficult task, but you will succeed if you persevere, and you will find a joy in overcoming obstacles – a delight in climbing rugged paths, which you would perhaps never know if you did not sometimes slip backward – if the road was always smooth and pleasant. Remember, no effort that we make to attain something beautiful is ever lost. Sometime, somewhere, somehow we shall find that which we seek. We shall speak, yes, and sing, too, as God intended we should speak and sing.

HELEN KELLER
1880–1968, born on this day; became deaf and blind
at the age of 19 months

June 28th⋆

The flowers left thick at nightfall in the wood
This Eastertide call into mind the men,
Now far from home, who, with their sweethearts, should
Have gathered them and will do never again.[111]

EDWARD THOMAS
1878–1917

⋆ World War I officially ended on this day in 1919 with the signing of the Treaty of Versailles.

June 29th

Teach us, O God, that when our fetters seem too
strong to break, the time has come at last when we
must break them.[112]

A. POWELL DAVIES
1902–1957, Unitarian minister, Washington, DC

June 30th

We give thanks for this season of roses and swifts,
of journeys and long, slow dusks,
of cool breezes and welcome showers,

holding on to this precious moment lightly,
and letting it go like a breath,
gently floating into pixels of light.

CAROLINE BLAIR
Kensington Unitarian, died September 2015

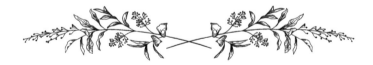

JULY

July 1st

I would love to say that I live a completely 'green' life; but if I did, I would be a liar. … But if we wait until we can do everything, it will be far too late. … Giving up meat is one of the easy things that almost anyone in the first world can do to become more impact-neutral in environmental terms. I make other choices about what I buy, and how I live, for similar reasons. For instance, my electricity is bought from a renewable-energy company; I buy second-hand whenever I can for things like furniture and books; I support small, local businesses rather than multinational corporations whenever possible, and buy as many organic and/or fair-trade variants of the things I need as I can afford. … There is a supermarket that I can walk to, so most of the time I use it instead of driving to an alternative, even though it means that I go more often.[113]

ALEX BRIANSON
Unitarian academic and activist

July 2nd

If the only prayer you said in your whole life was 'thank you', that would be enough.

MEISTER ECKHART

1260–1327, German theologian, philosopher, and mystic

July 3rd

We commune too much, O God, with what defeats us. We brood over our failures until failure takes possession of our hearts. Help us to see the good that we have done and to be encouraged by it. Help us to see the good we might have done and to be drawn towards it.[114]

A. POWELL DAVIES

1902–1957, Unitarian minister

July 4th

This is what you should do:
Love the earth and sun and animals,
despise riches, give alms to those who ask,
stand up for the stupid and crazy,
devote your income and labour to others,
hate tyrants, argue not concerning God,
have patience and indulgence towards people,
re-examine all that you have been told in school
    or church or any book,
dismiss what insults your very soul,
and your flesh shall become a great poem.[115]

WALT WHITMAN
1819–1892, American poet and essayist

July 5th

Waiting is difficult for many people, including me. I get
impatient in long queues. I groan when I just miss the
green traffic signal, and I sigh when my husband does
not answer my question immediately. Zen teachers say:
"When you are most tempted to do something, don't."
This is probably good advice. ... In the words of Reinhold
Niebuhr: "Just because we do nothing does not mean
that nothing is being done".[116]

JOHANNA BOEKE
Unitarian minister, retired

July 6th

God does not love one living being more than another, he loves all equally. God does not love one religion more than another, he loves all equally. So you should show equal kindness to all the living beings in your care. And you should show equal respect to all religions. You may practise whichever religion you wish, in the manner that suits you: but never despise the religions that others practise.

From THE BAGHAVAD GITA

July 7th

The Kingdom of God is inside you and all around you, not in buildings of wood and stone. Split a piece of wood and I am there. Turn a stone and you will find me.

THE GOSPEL OF THOMAS
Coptic version, found in Nag Hamadi in 1945

July 8th

Open our eyes so we may recognise that of God in all those we meet. … Open our ears to hear other people's life stories and, through hearing, understand them better. … Open our mouths to speak words of friendship and kindness to strangers. … Open our arms to help to tear down the barriers of fear that divide one group from another. … Open our minds to think bigger, braver thoughts and go beyond our narrow prejudices. … Open our hearts so love may flow through us, creating this world as one community which rejoices in people's diversity and encourages the inclusion of all.[117]

SARAH TINKER
Unitarian minister, Kensington

July 9th

Grant us to walk in beauty, seeing the uncommon in the common, aware of the great stream of wonder in which we and all things move. Give us to see more deeply into the great things of our heritage, and the simple but sublime truths hidden in every leaf and every rock. May our hands treat with respect the things which You have created. May we walk with other creatures as sharers with them in the one life that flows from You.[118]

JACOB TRAPP
1899–1992, Unitarian Universalist minister

July 10th

When all thoughts are exhausted
I slip into the wood and gather
A pile of shepherd's purse.
Like the little stream making its way
Through the mossy crevices
I, too, quietly turn clear and transparent.

RYOKAN
c.1758–1831, Japanese hermit monk

July 11th

All religions seek to demonstrate the reality of God
through symbols. These symbols are seen as pointers to
a transcendent reality beyond themselves. Symbols are
necessary, for they make the reality present to us. Every
word we use is a symbol. God is a symbol. Allah is a
symbol. Yahweh is a symbol. Christ is a symbol. These are
symbols we use to point to something which cannot be
described or expressed. The use of symbols points to the
mystery of human life: that is, that we are pushed beyond
ourselves, beyond our limits. ... Each religion has its
sacred and revered symbols. A contemplative awareness
will take us beyond all these to the one reality with which
we seek unity.[119]

BEDE GRIFFITHS
1906–1993, Benedictine monk and yogi, aka Swami Dayananda

July 12th

For age is opportunity no less
Than youth itself, though in another dress,
And as the evening twilight fades away
The sky is filled with stars, invisible by day.

HENRY WADSWORTH LONGFELLOW
1807–1882, American Unitarian poet

July 13th

Life is a gift which we have not earned and for which
we cannot pay. There is no necessity that there be a
universe, no inevitability about a world moving towards
life and then self-awareness. There might have been …
nothing at all. Since we have not earned J. S. Bach – or
friends or crocuses – the best we can do is to express
our gratitude for the undeserved gifts, and do our share
of the work of creation.[120]

ROBERT R. WALSH
1937–2016, Unitarian Universalist minister

July 14th

We may not have revelations like the apostles of old, we may not have experiences as the poets sing of, but we all have solemn times and seasons when the grandeur of the universe opens itself to our view; when we seem to be overwhelmed by the majestic harmony of the world in which we live, when the sea and air and sky seem to call forth in us infinite longings for a 'world not realized'. Yes, and there are those moments when we withdraw within ourselves – in the hush and silence of the night – when we review the past, remembering our successes and failures. When we realize how we have fallen short of the ideals of our youth and the aspirations of adulthood. Ah, friends, here and now let us look to the Infinite and the Eternal, whom no-one has seen at any time, except through the inspirations of beauty and the intuitions of the heart.[121]

GERTRUD VON PETZOLD

1876-1952, Unitarian, the first woman minister in any English denomination

July 15th

The Perfect Way is only difficult for those who pick and choose. Do not like, do not dislike: all will then be clear. Make a hairbreadth of difference, and Heaven and Earth are set apart. If you want truth to stand clear before you, never be for or against. The struggle between "like" and "dislike" is the mind's worst disease. While this deep meaning is misunderstood, it is useless to meditate on tranquillity. The Buddha-nature is featureless as space: it has no "too little" or "too much". Only because we take and reject does it seem to us not to be so.[122]

SENG-TS'AN, THE THIRD PATRIARCH
OF CHINESE ZEN BUDDHISM

July 16th

O God, may Thy Spirit help us to love our time,
to honour our fellows, to love and trust the world.
In Thy mercy, O God, help us to make sense of life,
to make sense of the world, to make sense of ourselves.

ARTHUR BENJAMIN DOWNING
1915–1980, Unitarian minister

July 17th

Let us give thanks for our many gifts by naming our blessings quietly to ourselves in these moments of stillness. ... Recognising our woes and faults, let us sit quietly with those parts of ourselves which cause us discomfort, in a spirit of gentle understanding and forgiveness. ... Spirit of the divine self, we open our hearts to listen to the wisdom of the still, small voice that may speak in these quiet moments. ... God of our hearts, let this small act of worship send a ripple of loving kindness from this place to our loved ones, our acquaintances, and the wider world.[123]

KATE DEAN
Unitarian minister, Rosslyn Hill Chapel, Hampstead

July 18th

There is only one breath. All are made of the same clay. Light within all is the same.

GURU GOBINDH SINGH
1666–1708, Sikh spiritual master

July 19th

An existential revolution should provide hope of a moral reconstitution of society, which means a radical renewal of the relationship of human beings to what I have called the human order, which no political order can replace.

A new experience of being, a renewed rootedness in the universe, a newly grasped sense of higher responsibility, a new-found inner relationship to other people and to the human community – these factors clearly indicate the direction in which we must go.[124]

VÁCLAV HAVEL
1936–2011, writer, dissident, first President of the Czech Republic

July 20th

The first gulp from the glass of natural sciences will make you an atheist, but at the bottom of the glass God is waiting for you.

WERNER HEISENBERG
Pioneer of quantum physics, 1901–1976

July 21st

When I open my eyes to the outer world, I feel myself as a drop in the sea. But when I close my eyes and look within, I see the whole universe as a bubble raised in the ocean of my heart.

HAZRAT INAYAT KHAN
Teacher of Universal Sufism, 1882–1927

July 22nd

Yesterday is done. Tomorrow never comes. Today is here. If you don't know what to do, sit still and listen. You may hear something. Nobody knows. We may pull apart the petals of a rose or make chemical analysis of its perfume, but the mystic beauty of its form and odor is still a secret, locked in to where we have no keys.[125]

CARL SANDBURG
1878–1967, Unitarian Universalist poet and Pulitzer Prize winner, died on this day

July 23rd

The same stream of life that runs through my veins night and day runs through the world and dances in rhythmic measures. It is the same life that shoots in joy through the dust of the earth in numberless blades of grass and breaks into tumultuous waves of leaves and flowers. It is the same life that is rocked in the ocean-cradle of birth and of death, in ebb and in flow.

I feel my limbs are made glorious by the touch of this world of life.

And my pride is from the life-throb of ages dancing in my blood this moment.[126]

RABINDRANATH TAGORE
1861–1941, Bengali poet and musician

July 24th

Defoe says that there were a hundred thousand country fellows in his time ready to fight to the death against popery, without knowing whether popery was a man or a horse.[127]

WILLIAM HAZLITT

1778–1830, Unitarian essayist and critic

July 25th

A rabbi asked his disciples, "How do you know that night has ended and the day is returning?" One disciple answered, "Is it when you see an animal in the distance and can tell whether it is a sheep or a dog?" "No", the rabbi replied. Another disciple asked "Is it when you look at a tree in the distance and can tell whether it is a fig or an olive tree?" "No", replied the rabbi. "It is when you look on the face of any man or woman and see that he or she is your brother or sister. If you cannot do this, no matter what the time, it is still night."

A JEWISH STORY

July 26th

A man can fail many times, but he isn't a failure until he begins to blame somebody else.

JOHN BURROUGHS

1837–1921, American naturalist and essayist

July 27th

When you apologise to someone, you are restoring
the dignity that you have violated in the person you
have hurt. You are also acknowledging that the offence
has happened. You are taking responsibility for your
part in causing harm. When you apologise with humility
and with true remorse for hurting another, you open
a space for healing. ... When you apologise, do it from
the heart. If you don't feel it, don't say it. It is only
when we recognise the suffering of the other person,
and the true harm we have caused, that our apologies
will be genuine. [128]

DESMOND TUTU
Former Archbishop of Capetown

July 28th

O God we praise you for our sense of hearing.
For comforting sounds: the ticking of clocks and
the purring of cats ... For homely sounds: a bubbling
saucepan full of good soup, and clean water flowing from
the tap ... For the sounds of nature: birds singing, bees
hunting honey, and the patter of raindrops ... For human
sounds: the powerful cry of the newborn baby, friends
talking, children playing ... For mechanical sounds:
the revving of a car engine, and a plane flying overhead.
And we thank You for our ability to listen, especially
to hear music of every sort: the organ here in chapel,

African drums, trombones and trumpets, a choir,
a string quartet. And we thank God for all those who
make music for us to share.[129]

JOSEPHINE SECCOMBE
Oxford Unitarian

July 29th

O God, from whom we ask so much and in our hearts
expect so little, show us that most of what we need is
ours already, if only we would take it. ... Remind us often,
O God, how much of our lives we are not living.[130]

A. POWELL DAVIES
1902–1957, Unitarian minister

July 30th

He is the source of light in all luminous objects.
He is beyond the darkness of matter and is unmanifested.
He is knowledge, He is the object of knowledge, and He
   is the goal of knowledge.
He is situated in everyone's heart.

THE BHAGAVAD GITA

July 31st

The shapes and colours of flowers and fruit, the curling
of a wave or a tendril, the songs of birds, the graceful
movements of living creatures, the regularity of a crystal
or a snowflake – all these and many more things are part
of the beauty of the world. It is this which enables us to
face up to the ugliness and pain of the world, which also
is a continuing feature of it. All things grow misshapen,
including human lives. There is grace, and there is also
distortion; there is sweetness and bitterness; there is
wonderful creativeness and there is senseless destruction.
And so we pray that we may learn to live in such a world,
and with such a human nature. We are grateful for all the
help and inspiration we receive from the frequent beauty
of the world, and the frequent grace in human lives.[131]

HARRY LISMER SHORT
1906–1975, Unitarian Principal of Manchester College Oxford

AUGUST

August 1st

Praised be my Lord God with all his creatures,
and especially our brother the sun,
who brings us the day and who brings us the light;
    fair is he and shines with a great splendour.
Praised be my Lord for our sister the moon, and for
    the stars,
the which he has set clear and lovely in the heavens.
Praised be my Lord for our sister water,
who is very serviceable unto us, and humble and
    precious and clean.
Praised be my Lord for our brother fire,
through whom Thou givest us light in the darkness;
    and he is bright and pleasant and very mighty and strong.
Praised be my Lord for our mother the earth,
the which doth sustain us and keep us, and bringeth forth
    divers fruit, and flowers of many colours, and grass. ...

ST FRANCIS OF ASSISI
1181–1226

August 2nd

Spend your brief moment according to nature's law, and
serenely greet the journey's end, as an olive falls when it
is ripe, blessing the branch that bore it, and giving thanks
to the tree that gave it life.

MARCUS AURELIUS
Stoic philosopher and Emperor of Rome from 161 to 180

August 3rd

To worship is to stand in awe under a heaven of stars,
before a flower, a leaf in sunlight, or a grain of sand.
To worship is to be silent, receptive, before a tree astir
    with the wind,
or the passing shadow of a cloud.
To worship is to work with dedication and skill;
it is to pause from work and listen to a strain of music.
To worship is to sing with the singing beauty of the earth;
it is to listen through a storm to the still small voice within.[132]

JACOB TRAPP
1899–1992, Unitarian Universalist minister

August 4th

Have mercy on me, O Beneficent One. I was angered for
I had no shoes. Then I met a man who had no feet.

TRADITIONAL CHINESE SAYING

August 5th

Let us think what some books have done for the world,
and what they are doing; how they keep up our hope,
awaken new courage and faith, soothe pain, give an ideal
life to those whose hours are cold and hard, bind together
distant ages and foreign lands, create new worlds of
beauty, bring down truth from heaven. We give eternal
blessings for this gift, and thank God for books.

JAMES FREEMAN CLARKE
1810–1888, Unitarian theologian and writer

I sit with a book,
And suddenly the miracle of being able to read
Hits me: words leap and prance,
Sing and dance, in the jazzy ecstacy of understanding.[133]

ELIZABETH ROGERS (BIRTLES)
Unitarian minister, retired

August 6th

"Miracles have ceased." Have they indeed? When?
They had not ceased this afternoon when I walked into
the wood and got into bright, miraculous sunshine,
in shelter from the roaring wind.

RALPH WALDO EMERSON
1803–1882, Unitarian minister, essayist, and philosopher
in Boston, Massachusetts

August 7th

Let us have the presence to stand at the edge of the sea
To sense the ebb and flow of the tides.
Let us have the senses to feel the breath of a mist
moving over a great saltmarsh,
To watch the flight of shore birds
that have swept up and down the continents
For untold thousands of years,
and see the endless running of the eels to the sea.
Let us have the knowledge of things that are as
    nearly eternal
as any earthly life can be.[134]

RACHEL CARSON
Words adapted for prayer by Bert Clough (Oxford Unitarian)

August 8th

Out of the loose ends of this life we must make a coherent plan of living. We must purify our hearts and simplify our affections, so that God's grace may flow through us and make our lives fruitful and good. Each of us has some problem of living which weighs heavily on our heart. Usually it is a problem of human relationships: how ought we to deal with this – or that – fellow human being? …
We pray for wisdom and patience, justice and kindness – not that we may have a complete answer to our questions, but that we may see before us a way of living. [135]

HARRY LISMER SHORT
1906–1975, Unitarian Principal of Manchester College Oxford

August 9th

The sanest man sets up no deed, lays down no law,
Takes everything that happens as it comes,
As something to animate, not to appropriate,
To earn, not to own,
To accept naturally without self-importance:
If you never assume importance,
You never lose it. [136]

LAO TZU
BCE 604–BCE 531, Chinese philosopher, author of the Tao Te Ching

August 10th

We must be ready to recognise the interests of others,
even when they run counter to our own. But the person
who does that does not really sacrifice himself, but
becomes a larger self.

JOHN DEWEY
1859–1952, Unitarian philosopher, psychologist, and educational reformer

August 11th

No man is an island entire of itself; every man is a
piece of the continent, a part of the main; if a clod be
washed away by the sea, Europe is the less, as well as if
a promontory were, as well as any manor of thy friend's
or of thine own were; any man's death diminishes me,
because I am involved in mankind. And therefore never
send to know for whom the bell tolls; it tolls for thee.[137]

JOHN DONNE
1572-1631, metaphysical poet and Dean of St Paul's Cathedral

August 12th

Activity is better than inertia.
Act, but with self-control.
The world is imprisoned in its own activity,
except when actions are performed as worship of God.
Therefore you must perform every action sacramentally.

THE BHAGAVAD GITA

August 13th

The martyr sacrifices herself (himself in a few instances)
entirely in vain. Or rather not in vain; for she (or he)
makes the selfish more selfish, the lazy more lazy,
the narrow narrower.[138]

FLORENCE NIGHTINGALE
*1820–1910, social reformer, statistician, founder of modern nursing;
raised as a Unitarian; born on this day*

August 14th

Let us be still and listen for all the sounds around us …
The noise of passing traffic, the steps of passers-by; a
distant train or a barking dog; an aeroplane overhead …
The wind in the leaves, the rattle of branches; the
singing of birds, the patter of rain; the rustle of
autumn leaves or the quiet of winter snow …

The creak of a chair, the tick of a clock, the sound of our
own breathing, the beating of our own hearts.
Let us listen to the sounds within us, sounds known
only to ourselves …

The unspoken noise of our own tumbling thoughts,
the silent shouting of our own feelings …
The cascading pictures in our own minds' eyes – all
disturbing our quiet. Let us be still within.
Let us listen to a stillness deeper within us. Let us listen
to the voice of inner silence.
Let us be still and know that God is here.[139]

SYDNEY H. KNIGHT
1923–2004, Unitarian minister and hymn writer

August 15th

If we don't feel grateful for what we already have,
what makes us think we'd be happy with more?

(From the website of the Banbury Unitarian Fellowship)

August 16th

In this quiet place, O God, help us to find quiet for our
souls. For we need quietness. Shouting and tumult are
always about us, and the noise of the world never dies
down. Even in the night-time when we seek rest, the
voices of the day go on. But in your presence, there
is quietness. O God, let us find your presence now![140]

A. POWELL DAVIES
1902–1957, Unitarian minister

August 17th

*How could we sleep at all unless we gave absolution, each to our
own self and also to all others, every night of our lives?*

Johann Wolfgang von Goethe

In our own sense of the Highest and Holiest, let us now in
silence face our own shortcomings and failures, and those
we find in others; looking first into our own depths and
then at the life around us, facing honestly the inevitable
imperfection of being human. … Let us now, in some
awareness of weakness or sin or failure, in ourselves

and in others, recognise our need to forgive and to be forgiven; in silence of heart and mind forgive ourselves and others who need our forgiveness; and be open to receive forgiveness human and divine. ... O Holy One, we need your presence in and around us, to know ourselves in both weakness and strength, to find forgiveness for ourselves, to renew our faith and love, to live better lives in ourselves and among others.[141]

BRUCE FINDLOW
Unitarian minister, Principal of Manchester College Oxford 1974–1985

August 18th

God is not a watchmaker who then periodically tinkers with the creation he long ago established. Instead, God is one with all that exists. The great miracle is the energizing force of the universe itself. One mind is everywhere active, in each ray of the star, in each wavelet of the pool.

RALPH WALDO EMERSON
1803–1882, Unitarian minister, essayist, and philosopher, Boston, Massachusetts

August 19th

Does the commandment "Thou Shalt Not Kill" mean nothing to us? Are we to interpret it as meaning "Thou shalt not kill except on the grand scale", or "Thou shalt not kill except when the national leaders say to do so"?[142]

LINUS PAULING
*1901–1994, Unitarian Universalist, awarded Nobel Prizes
for Chemistry and Peace, died on this day*

August 20th

Silence is the gift of music
when its closing cadence dies
in hush of adoration.

Silence is fulfilment of desire
that ends its asking
to find true prayer unspoken.

Silence is the benediction
that stills the day's debate
by speaking the Eternal Word.[143]

MARJORIE EASTON
1910–1989, Unitarian minister

August 21st

What exactly is an angel? Here is how I suggest we
can tell if we bump into one. Angels deny that they *are*
angels. They don't all have wings or halos – those are
only the ones who like to dress up. Angels don't expect
anything in return for services rendered. They don't
always tell us what we want to hear. … Angels aren't all
called Michael or Gabriel. We might even be angels and
not realise it. … Yes, angels are here among us, giving us
gifts beyond measure. Gifts of humour when we think
the sun will never shine again, passion when we believe
we are unlovable, inspiration when our life force wanes,
confidentiality when we can't tell anyone else our secrets,
forgiveness when we so sorely need it, advice when we
don't know which direction to turn, frankness when we
try to tell less than the truth about who we really are, and
the gift of just being there when we are so very alone.[144]

DON BEAUDREAULT
Unitarian Universalist minister, retired

August 22nd

We cannot tell the precise moment when friendship is
formed. As in filling a vessel drop by drop, there is at last a
drop which makes it run over; so in a series of kindnesses
there is at last one which makes the heart run over.[145]

RAY BRADBURY
1920–2012, Unitarian Universalist science fiction writer, born on this day

August 23rd

The more we lose our sense of separateness in the
knowledge of the one-ness of all living creatures, millions
of small leaves on the one single tree of life, the more
we shall lose our sense of self-importance, and so be
liberated from our self-pity: a bondage so horrible that
I believe it can bring us at last to a state not unlike that
of Gollum, the dreadful creature that Tolkien created,
living alone in the dark, talking to himself, murmuring
"My preciouss. My preciouss."… But if we can find a little
of our one-ness with all other creatures, and love them,
then I believe we are half-way towards finding God.[146]

ELIZABETH GOUDGE
1900–1984, novelist and children's author

August 24th

Above all, try to be kind. I have no doubt that kindness
is the greatest virtue. You can find a million reasons in
any one day to dislike people, to feel resentment or even
loathing. But to be kind is to protect yourself from the
worst parts of your own nature. You may fear that to face
people with an open heart leaves you vulnerable, open to
abuse. I rather doubt it. The way of the hard face is much
harder. Be kind to others, especially the more difficult
people you encounter, and that kindness will come
back to you.[147]

FEARGAL KEANE
Journalist, writer, broadcaster

August 25th

The goodness of God fills all the gaps of the universe, without discrimination or preference. God is the gratuity of absolutely everything. The space in between everything is not space at all, but Spirit. God is the "Goodness Glue" that holds the dark and light of things together, the free energy that carries all death across the Great Divide and transmutes it into Life. … *Grace is what God does to keep all things God has made in love and alive forever.* Grace is God's official job description. Grace is not something God gives; grace is who God is. If we are to believe the primary witnesses, an unexplainable goodness is at work in the universe.[148]

RICHARD ROHR
Franciscan priest, New Mexico

August 26th

The Jesus that we meet in the gospels is not asking us to bow down and worship him: he is asking us to walk alongside him and to bear witness with him to the presence of God in the beauty and mystery of the world and in the decency and dignity of human persons. The Jesus we meet in the serenity and grace of the worship space is not calling us to bear witness to his own glory; he is calling us to bear witness to the love of God in the extraordinary lives of ordinary people, to the presence of God within us all.[149]

TOM MCCREADY
Unitarian minister, Hull

August 27th

The medieval Christian mystic Meister Eckhart
suggests that if the only prayer we say in our lifetime
is "thank you", that would suffice. ... Saying thank you
to the Great Provider is only one part of a life of
gratitude. ... Say thank you to somebody who least
expects it from you today. Gratitude paid to all around
us becomes a spiritual exercise. Show your gratitude to
the music that enchants, to the winter boots that stand
up to the wear and tear of the elements, to the movie
that brings tears to your eyes. ... Feast on the moments
that stand out in your mind as precious enough to replay
again and again.[150]

FREDERIC and MARY ANN BRUSSATT

August 28th

Our deepest fear is not that we are inadequate.
Our deepest fear is that we are powerful beyond
measure. It is our light, not our darkness, that most
frightens us. We ask ourselves, Who am I to be brilliant,
gorgeous, talented, fabulous? Actually, who are you
not to be? You are a child of God. Your playing small
does not serve the world. There's nothing enlightened
about shrinking so that other people won't feel insecure
around you. We are all meant to shine, as children do.
We were born to make manifest the glory of God that
is within us. It's not just in some of us; it's in everyone.
And as we let our own light shine, we unconsciously

give other people permission to do the same. As we're liberated from our own fear, our presence automatically liberates others.[151]

MARIANNE WILLIAMSON
Author, lecturer, campaigner

August 29th

Spirit of beauty, whose revelations come to us in
    sun and rain, dawn and dusk,
In all flowing, circling, shining and living things,
And in the quiet at the heart of all motion,
Be within us this day as the wonder and welcome
    of the living soul.
Awaken our senses and quicken our minds
That we may partake, and be inwardly fed and renewed.
May we give our hearts to beauty,
As the harp gives itself to the hand.
May we turn towards the true and the good,
As buds and flowers are uplifted to the sun.[152]

JACOB TRAPP
1899–1992, Unitarian Universalist minister

August 30th

None of us is required to belong to a faith group.
No one is policing our religious thoughts. Yet we
Unitarians choose to be in community, to look at the
mysteries of life, to support one another, and to pray.
And we do it without the certainty offered by dogma,
created inside high walls.[153]

COLLEEN BURNS
Editor of The Inquirer

August 31st

Let us be grateful for the love and support of friends;
and for chance encounters that have proved helpful;
and for strangers who have met our needs in times of
crisis, not seeking anything in return. In all these we
may glimpse, if we choose, the love of God working
in our lives … Let us be grateful for temptations we have
overcome, difficulties we have surmounted, pain and
hurt we have been able to rise above. In all these we
may glimpse, if we choose, the power of God at work
in our lives.[154]

RICHARD LOVIS
Unitarian writer and lay leader; deceased

SEPTEMBER

September 1st

O God, to whom we pray for truth, be with us in our
trembling lest we find it. We fear its light; our lives are
full of shadows: what shall we do for shelter when we
stand before the brightness of truth? We do not want the
truth that troubles us and seeks to save us; we look for
truth that brings us safety, comfort, and repose. … We
do not want the truth that tells us of a world of human
wretchedness, with wrongs to be set right and justice
calling us to serve it. For if we see this truth, we must
admit our own betrayals: our callousness and cowardice,
our evasions and our love of ease. We do not seek the
truth of conscience. We want an indulgent God of
tenderness and loving kindness who will not trouble
our conscience or challenge our complacency. Forgive
us our complacency, O God.[155]

A. POWELL DAVIES
1902–1957, Unitarian minister

September 2nd

What kind of religion is this Unitarianism? It is humanity lightened by divinity. It is humanism and theism combined. It is not the kind of humanism without God and without a soul, but the humanism of those great individuals who from time to time called our nation to a new life. … What else is it but to begin with humankind when seeking God?[156]

NORBERT ČAPEK

1870–1942, founder of the Czech Unitarian church, died at Dachau

September 3rd

Advice to his daughters: Your job as a citizen and as a decent human being is to constantly affirm and fight for treating people with kindness and respect and understanding. And you should anticipate that at any given moment there are going to be flare-ups of bigotry that you may have to confront, or maybe inside you, and you have to vanquish them.[157]

BARACK OBAMA

Forty-fourth President of the United States, 2009–2017

September 4th

To have the ability to withdraw into oneself and forget everything around one when one is creating: that, I think, is the only requirement for being able to bring forth something beautiful. The whole thing is a mystery.

EDVARD GRIEG
Unitarian composer, died on this day in 1907

September 5th

Can I see another's woe,
and not be in sorrow too?
Can I see another's grief,
and not seek for kind relief?[158]

WILLIAM BLAKE
1757–1827

September 6th

For what is prayer but the expansion of yourself into the living ether? And if it is for your comfort to pour your darkness into space, it is also for your delight to pour forth the dawning of your heart ... When you pray, you rise to meet in the air those who are praying at that very hour, and whom – save in prayer – you may not meet.[159]

KAHLIL GIBRAN
1883–1931, Lebanese-American writer and artist

September 7th

Over the infinity of space and time, the infinitely more infinite love of God comes to possess us. He comes at his own time. We have the power to consent to receive him or to refuse. If we remain deaf, he comes back again and again like a beggar, but also, like a beggar, one day he stops coming. If we consent, God puts a little seed in us and he goes away again. From that moment God has no more to do; neither have we, except to wait. ... On the whole, however, the seed grows itself. A day comes when the soul belongs to God, when it not only consents to love but when truly and effectively it loves. Then in turn it must cross the universe to go to God.[160]

SIMONE WEIL

1909–1943, French philosopher, mystic, and political activist

September 8th

When I injure any kind of life, I must be quite certain that it is necessary. I must never go beyond the unavoidable, not even in apparently insignificant things. The farmer who has mowed down a thousand flowers in his meadow in order to feed his cattle must be careful on his way home not to strike the head off a single flower by the side of the road in idle amusement, for he infringes on the law of life without being under the pressure of necessity.[161]

ALBERT SCHWEITZER

1875–1965, philosopher, musician, and doctor; member of the Unitarian Universalist Church of the Larger Fellowship

September 9th

Give us grace, O God, to be grateful sometimes for the things we take for granted, the common courtesies of life and the kindness that is shown us. When we complain that we are carrying heavy burdens, let us see that others share them, often carrying the greater part of the load.[162]

A. POWELL DAVIES
1902–1957, Unitarian minister

September 10th

I cannot bear to think of being no more – of losing myself – though existence is often but a painful consciousness of misery; nay, it appears to me impossible that I should cease to exist, or that this active, restless spirit, equally alive to joy and sorrow, should be only organized dust – ready to fly abroad the moment the spring snaps, or the spark goes out, which kept it together. Surely something resides in this heart that is not perishable – and life is more than a dream.

MARY WOLLSTONECRAFT
Unitarian feminist and writer, died on this day in 1797

September 11th

A human being is part of the whole called by us the
Universe, a part limited in time and space. We experience
ourselves, our thoughts and feelings as something separate
from the rest. A kind of optical delusion of consciousness.
This delusion is a kind of prison for us, restricting us to our
personal desires and to affection for a few persons nearest
to us. Our task must be to free ourselves from the prison
by widening our circle of compassion to embrace all living
creatures and the whole of nature in its beauty. The true
value of a human being is determined by the measure
and the sense in which they have obtained liberation from
the self. We shall require a substantially new manner of
thinking if humanity is to survive.[163]

ALBERT EINSTEIN
1879–1955, theoretical physicist

September 12th

These fellow-mortals, every one, must be accepted as they
are: you can neither straighten their noses, nor brighten
their wit, nor rectify their dispositions; and it is these
people – amongst whom your life is passed – that it is
needful you should tolerate, pity, and love: it is these more
or less ugly, stupid, inconsistent people whose moments
of goodness you should be able to admire – for whom you
should cherish all possible hopes, all possible patience.[164]

GEORGE ELIOT (MARY ANN EVANS)
*1819–1880; novelist; associated with the Rosslyn Hill
Unitarian congregation, Hampstead*

September 13th

Eternal Spirit, look kindly upon us as we struggle to make sense of the experiences that have happened to us. Forgive our weakness when our memories are so painful that we turn away from experiences that we cannot yet face. Grant us the serenity eventually to find the strength to come to terms with our bitterest memories … May we always remember that in our dealings with other people we may be creating memories for them, and may we never have cause to regret the memory that we leave in their heart.[165]

HOWARD WILKINS
Member of the Hinckley Great Meeting Unitarian congregation

September 14th

Divine Spirit, give us the strength
to act honourably and respectfully
towards the earth and all her creatures,
including our own species.
Give us the power to act now, and
let co-operation, not competition,
be our default mode of being.
Amen.[166]

MARIA CURTIS
Unitarian minister, Horsham

September 15th

There are barriers which divide the righteous and
the unrighteous. But we know that each of us is both.
There is within us the impulse to be generous, kind,
worthy, and decent. And there is within us the impulse
to be cruel, mean-spirited, and vengeful. Help us not to
see people, ourselves included, as either one thing nor
the other, but to recognise that we are all complex and
imperfect creatures, and that acknowledging the fullness
of our humanity shared with all beings is one way
to break down the walls.[167]

DAVID USHER
Unitarian minister

September 16th

Looking back upon the year's accumulated heap of
troubles, Margaret wondered how they had been borne.
If she could have anticipated them, how she would have
shrunk away and hid herself from the coming time!
And yet day by day had, of itself, and by itself, been very
endurable – small, keen, bright little spots of positive
enjoyment having come sparkling into the very middle
of sorrows.[168]

ELIZABETH GASKELL
Unitarian novelist, 1810–1865

September 17th

God of life and love, encountered in the generosity of
the good earth and in the hearts of generous men and
women: we give thanks this day for our dear mother the
earth, who sustains us and keeps us, as she sails through
space like some beautiful pearl of greatest price. ... We
give thanks for those who work on the land: the farmers
of the fields and the fishers of the seas; those who sweat
and toil beneath the earth for her hidden riches; those who
labour in factory or office, in business, in law, in teaching,
in government, in the care of the sick; in the care and
upbringing of children; so that the riches of this land may
be dealt out to all, justly and rightly. ... Glory to God in
the highest, and on earth peace, goodwill to all people.[169]

FRANK WALKER
Unitarian minister, retired

September 18th

A sound man's heart is not shut within itself,
But is open to other people's hearts:
I find good people good,
And I find bad people good, if I am good enough.
I trust men of their word,
And I trust liars, if I am true enough.
I feel the heartbeats of others above my own
If I am enough of a father, enough of a son.[170]

LAO TZU
BCE 604–BCE 531, Chinese philosopher, author of the Tao Te Ching

September 19th

An agnostic friend of mine eventually converted to the Catholic faith. She received religious instruction from a devout and simple-minded nun. They were discussing the story of the Annunciation, which presented some difficulties to my friend. At last she said to the nun, "Well, anyhow, I suppose that one is not obliged to believe that the Blessed Virgin was visited by a solid angel, dressed in a white robe?" To this the nun replied doubtfully, "No, dear, perhaps not. But still, you know, he would have to wear *something*."

Now here, it seems to me, we have a great theological truth. The elusive contacts and subtle realities of the world of spirit have got to wear something, if we are to grasp them at all. Moreover, they must wear something which is easily recognised by the human eye and human heart – more, by the primitive, half-conscious folk-soul existing in each one of us, stirring in the depths and reaching out in its own way towards God.[171]

EVELYN UNDERHILL

1875–1941, Anglo-Catholic writer on mysticism; Upton Lecturer on the Philosophy of Religion at Manchester College Oxford in 1921

September 20th

Let love continue. If we agree in love, there is no disagreement that can do us any injury; but if we do not, no other agreement can do us any good. Let us keep a secret guard against the enemy that sows discord among us. Let us endeavour to keep the unity of spirit in the bonds of peace.

HOSEA BALLOU
1771–1852, Universalist minister

September 21st

May we be blessed with discomfort
with easy answers, half-truths, and superficial relationships,
so that we may live deep within our hearts. …

And may we be blessed with enough foolishness
to believe that we can make a difference in this world,
so that we can do what others claim cannot be done.

A FRANCISCAN BLESSING

September 22nd★

I call that mind free which does not cower to human opinion; which refuses to be the slave or tool of the many or of the few, and guards its empire over itself as nobler than the empire of the world.

★ John Biddle, a Unitarian martyr, died in prison for his beliefs on this day in 1662.

I call that mind free which resists the bondage of habit, which does not mechanically copy the past, nor live on its old virtues; but listens for new and higher notions of conscience, and rejoices to pour itself forth in fresh and higher exertions.

I call that mind free which has cast off all fear but that of wrongdoing, and which no menace or peril can enthrall: which is calm in the midst of tumults, and possesses itself, though all else will be lost.[172]

WILLIAM ELLERY CHANNING
1780–1842, Unitarian minister and theologian, England and America

September 23rd

May I be at peace.
May my loved ones be at peace.
May those I have never met be at peace.
May those I have hurt, knowingly or unknowingly,
    be at peace.
May those who have hurt me, knowingly or
    unknowingly, be at peace.
May everybody be at peace.

BUDDHIST LOVING-KINDNESS MEDITATION
(METTA BHAVANA)

September 24th

Some say we get what we deserve in life, but I don't believe it. We certainly don't deserve J. S. Bach, for example. What have I done to deserve the Second Brandenburg Concerto? I have not been kind enough; I have not done enough justice; I have not loved my neighbour, or myself, sufficiently; I have not praised God enough to have earned a gift like this.[173]

ROBERT R. WALSH
1937–2016, Unitarian Universalist minister

September 25th

Some people are walking around with full use of their bodies – and they're more paralysed than I am.

CHRISTOPHER REEVE[*]
1952–2004, Unitarian Universalist; Superman *film star; born on this day*

September 26th

To be silent with another person is a deep expression of trust and confidence, and it is only when we are unconfident that we feel compelled to talk. To be silent with another person is truly to *be* with that other person. ...We do not have to create silence. The silence is there

---

[*] Paralysed from the neck down after a horse-riding accident in 1995. Founded the Christopher and Dana Reeve Foundation, in support of people living with disabilities.

within us. What we have to do is to become silent, to become the silence. The purpose of meditation is to allow ourselves to become silent enough to *allow* this interior silence to emerge. Silence is the language of the spirit.[174]

JOHN MAIN
1926–1982, Benedictine monk

September 27th

Not religion only, but unbiased common sense as well as accurate deductions of scientific research, lead to the conclusion that all mankind are one great family, of which numerous nations and tribes existing are only various branches. Hence enlightened men in all countries feel a wish to encourage and facilitate human intercourse in every manner by removing as far as possible all impediments to it, in order to promote reciprocal advantage and enjoyment of the whole human race.

RAJA RAM MOHUN ROY
Founder of the Brahmo Samaj 'One God Society', universalist,
internationalist, friend of Unitarians, died on this day in 1833

September 28th

Backward and forward, eternity is the same; already we have been the nothing we dread to be.[175]

HERMAN MELVILLE
Unitarian author of Moby Dick, *died on this day in 1891*

September 29th

There is no work in the world, except perhaps the slaughtering of other people, that a woman cannot do as efficiently as a man if she is given the same training and opportunity.[176]

GERTRUD VON PETZOLD

1876-1952, Unitarian, England's first woman minister in any denomination, began her ministry in Leicester on this day in 1904

September 30th

The spacious firmament on high,
With all the blue ethereal sky,
And spangled heavens, a shining frame,
Their great Original proclaim…
Soon as the evening shades prevail,
The moon takes up the wondrous tale,
And nightly to the listening earth
Repeats the story of her birth.

JOSEPH ADDISON

1672–1719

OCTOBER

October 1st

A gift is pure when it is given from the heart to the right person at the right time and at the right place, and when we expect nothing in return.

THE BHAGAVAD GITA

October 2nd

Worship God by reverencing the human soul as God's chosen sanctuary. Revere it in yourselves, revere it in others, and labour to carry it forward. … Go forth to respect the rights, and seek the true, enduring welfare of all within your influence. Carry with you the conviction that to trample on a human being, of whatever colour, clime, rank, condition, is to trample on God's child. … Go forth to do good with every power which God

bestows, to make every place you enter happier by your
presence, to espouse all human interests, to throw your
whole weight into the scale of human freedom and
improvement, to withstand all wrong, to uphold all
right, and especially to give light, life, strength to the
immortal soul.[177]

WILLIAM ELLERY CHANNING
1780–1842, Unitarian minister and theologian, died on this day in 1842

October 3rd

We often hear grown-up people complaining of having to
hang about a railway station and wait for a train. Did you
ever hear a small boy complain of having to hang about
a railway station and wait for a train? No; for to him to be
inside a railway station is to be inside a cavern of wonder
and a palace of poetical pleasures. Because to him the
red light and the green light on the signal are like a new
sun and a new moon. Because to him when the wooden
arm of the signal falls down suddenly, it is as if a great
king had thrown down his staff as a signal and started a
shrieking tournament of trains. I myself am of little boys'
habit in this matter. They also serve who only stand and
wait for the two-fifteen.[178]

G.K. CHESTERTON
1874–1936, Catholic writer, Unitarian parents

October 4th
World Animals Day
(The Feast Day of Francis of Assisi)

How it is that animals understand things I do not know, but it is certain that they do understand. Perhaps there is a language which is not made of words, and everything in the world understands it. Perhaps there is a soul hidden in everything and it can always speak, without even making a sound, to another soul.

FRANCES HODGSON BURNETT
1849–1924, children's writer, author of The Secret Garden

October 5th

Everything the power of the world does is done in a circle. The sky is round, and I have heard that the earth is round like a ball, and so are all the stars. The wind, in its greatest power, whirls. Birds make their nests in circles, for theirs is the same religion as ours. The sun comes forth and goes down again in a circle. The moon does the same, and both are round. Even the seasons form a great circle in their changing, and always come back again to where they were. The life of a man is a circle from childhood to childhood, and so it is in everything where power moves.[179]

BLACK ELK
1863–1950, a Native American holy man of the Oglala Lakota nation

October 6th

The question of God or Ultimate Reality is an open one for Unitarians. We know we are part of a cosmic reality greater than ourselves, but we are hard put to name it. For some it is God, for others Nature, or Cosmos, or Being itself. Some believe that to name it is to diminish it.

I am less concerned with answering that question and more concerned that religious liberals have experiences that may be called divine. ... It may be, for instance, that God is a verb, not a noun. That is, the word may not refer to any being *up there* or even *in there*, but to a divine *process* of which we are a part. It may be that we experience the divine in relational power – that it is created out of the gathering of people in worship or in pursuit of a noble cause.[180]

RICHARD S. GILBERT
Unitarian Universalist minister

October 7th

I do not see human beings as the ultimate crown of creation. Life forms do not constitute a pyramid with humans at the apex, but rather a circle where everything is connected and interdependent. We could not live without the rest of nature, but nature can carry on without us![181]

INGRID TAVKAR
Rosslyn Hill Unitarian congregation

October 8th

Whither shall I go from thy spirit? or whither shall I flee
from thy presence? If I ascend up into heaven, thou art
there: if I make my bed in hell, behold, thou art there.
If I take the wings of the morning, and dwell in the
uttermost parts of the sea, even there shall thy hand
lead me, and thy right hand shall hold me. If I say, Surely
the darkness shall cover me, even the night shall be light
about me. Yea, the darkness hideth not from thee; but
the night shineth as the day: the darkness and the light
are both alike to thee.

PSALM 139, VERSES 7−12
King James' Bible

October 9th

On earth there is a need for people who work more
and criticise less; who build more and destroy less;
who promise less and deliver more; who hope to receive
less and give more; who demand better today and
not tomorrow.[182]

CHE GUEVARA
Cuban physician and revolutionary; died on this day in 1967

October 10th

Eternal Spirit of Life and Love, green and dying is the world about us and the world within. Green is the world in the fullness of its beauty, green is the mind in the rich glories of the imagination. Green is the world in the birth of tree and flower, the springing into life of creatures great and small. Green is the mind in the continuous, surging reparation of the power of Love. Dying is our world as the leaves mulch to the land – even hills and forests and the great oceans come and go. Dying is the world within, as old delusions fail and memory impairs, and intellects, like limbs, lose their agility. But even in its dying the world fares green again, and even in our dying we may be born again, dying and rising many times before our end. [183]

CELIA MIDGLEY
Unitarian minister, retired

October 11th

Let us pay attention to our breathing.
Let us be relaxed in our bodies and our minds.
Let us be at peace with our bodies and our minds.
Let us return to ourselves and become wholly ourselves.
Let us be aware of the source of being that is common
    to us all, and to all living things.
Evoking the presence of the Great Compassion, let us fill our hearts with our own compassion – towards ourselves and towards all living beings. [184]

THE VENERABLE THICH NHAT HAHN
Vietnamese Buddhist monk and peace activist

October 12th

I have lived amidst eternity. Be grateful, my soul. My life was worth living. He who was pressed from all sides but remained victorious in spirit is welcomed into the choir of heroes. He who overcame the fetters giving wing to the mind is entering into the golden age of the victorious.

NORBERT ČAPEK

Czechoslovakian Unitarian minister,
gassed in the concentration camp at Dachau on this day in 1942

October 13th

I perceive the Divine as that which is within and that which connects me to the whole, as well as all that is. There is lack of separation and division when spirit speaks to spirit. It is the God within, the God between, and God the other. The Divine is the breath shared between me and creation. The Divine is wholeness. The Divine is the eternal energy of the world that flows through all. The Divine is Love. Without the Divine of many names there is no meaningful life.[185]

ANONYMOUS

Contributor to Unitarians: Together in Diversity

October 14th

Often when with deliberation
I set out to enjoy nature with a capital 'N',
my eagerness and expectation
lead to disappointment once again.
But if, without intent, I step outside
merely to hang my washing on the line,
I am completely overwhelmed by the fine
    October day:

the singing birds, the sparkling light,
the falling leaves put to flight
all introspection, I belong
to the simple life of the bird song
and sunlight and Autumn breeze,
And for a brief moment am at ease
in the world, disarmed into the peace
of the everyday.[186]

ANONYMOUS LAY BUDDHIST
Dedicated to the memory of Ayya Rocana, Amaravati Buddhist Centre

October 15th

Living Spirit of Love, we come before you in need of
your help. ... You would have us love our neighbour
as we love ourselves. You would even have us love our
enemies. But so often we have heard those words,
admired the sentiment, and then forgotten them.
Help us to love, O God, to get beneath the hatred and
the prejudice, the ignorance and the self-righteousness,
to see another human soul as weak as our own. ...
We ask this for the sake of our neighbours, our enemies,
and ourselves. Amen.[187]

CLIFF REED
Unitarian minister, retired

October 16th

Nonviolence requires of those who practise it, from
whatever religious or cultural background they may
come, an extraordinary commitment. It requires nothing
less than the transformation of ourselves. We have to
look deeply into our own anger, our aggressiveness
and our fear. It's no less arduous than training for the
Olympics. And the results are no less rewarding. When
you meet real peace-makers, they are radiant. They
radiate an inner spaciousness, a joy and a power that
is greater than any weapon.[188]

SCILLA ELWORTHY
International peace campaigner

October 17th

… if, as we work, we can transmit life into our work,
Life, still more life, rushes into us to compensate,
   to be ready,
And we ripple with life through the days.
Even if it is a woman making an apple dumpling,
   or a man a stool,
If life goes into the pudding, good is the pudding,
Good is the stool,
Content is the woman, with fresh life rippling in to her,
Content is the man.[189]

D. H. LAWRENCE

*1885–1930, poet, novelist, and one-time member of
the High Pavement Unitarian congregation in Nottingham*

October 18th

It is a splendid thing to think that the woman you really
love will never grow old to you. Through the wrinkles
of time, through the mask of years, if you really love
her, you will always see the face you loved and won.
And a woman who really loves a man does not see that
he grows old; he is not decrepit to her; he does not
tremble; he is not old; she always sees the same gallant
gentleman who won her hand and heart. I like to think
of it in that way; I like to think that love is eternal.
And to love in that way and then go down the hill
of life together, and as you go down, hear, perhaps,

the laughter of grandchildren, while the birds of joy and love sing once more in the leafless branches of the tree of age.[190]

ROBERT INGERSOLL

1833–1899, American political leader, orator, and Unitarian agnostic

October 19th

> We build on foundations we did not lay.
> We warm ourselves at fires we did not light.
> We sit in the shade of trees we did not plant.
> We drink from wells we did not dig.
> We profit from persons we did not know.
> We are ever bound in community.[191]

THE BOOK OF DEUTERONOMY, 6: 10–12,

adapted by Peter Raible

October 20th

I am the supreme and fiery force who kindled every living
spark … I am the fiery life of the essence of God: I flame
above the beauty of the fields; I shine in the waters;
I burn in the sun, the moon, and the stars. And, with
the airy wind, I quicken all things vitally by an unseen,
all-sustaining life….

I am Life…. Mine is the blast of the resounding Word
through which all creation came to be, and I quickened all
things with my breath … I am Life, whole and undivided
… all that lives has its root in Me.[192]

HILDEGARD OF BINGEN
1098–1179, Benedictine abbess, writer, composer, Christian mystic

October 21st

He prayeth well, who loveth well
both man and bird and beast.
He prayeth best, who loveth best
all things both great and small;
for the dear God who loveth us,
He made and loveth all.[193]

SAMUEL TAYLOR COLERIDGE
Poet and one-time Unitarian minister, born on this day in 1772

October 22nd

Having lived for years with the easy assumption that life
is for ever, being confronted with the realisation that
life in fact is finite requires some profound reflection
and adjustment of expectations. Not all people manage
the process well. Some go to their deaths protesting
and resentful, their spirits like children upset because a
favourite toy has been taken from them. Others enter into
a state of spiritual serenity, even joy, as they approach their
deaths. They let go of their tenacious grasp on life, and in
doing so their life assumes a new quality. ... At all times all
people are in the process of dying. We never know when
our time will come. ... Be willing to let go, and in letting
go you will find what you have sought.[194]

DAVID USHER
Unitarian minister

October 23rd

Nice distinctions are troublesome. It is so much easier
to say that a thing is black than to discriminate the
particular shade of brown, blue, or green to which it
really belongs. It is so much easier to make up your mind
that your neighbour is good for nothing, than to enter
into all the circumstances that would oblige you to
modify that opinion.[195]

GEORGE ELIOT (MARY ANN EVANS)
*1819–1880; novelist; associated with the
Rosslyn Hill Unitarian congregation, Hampstead*

October 24th

Stepping through the gate into Chatsworth Park early
this morning, I saw the yellow, brown, and golden leaves
quietly swirling to the ground, glinting in the sun that was
just breaking through the cold, damp mist of morning.
I crunched through the dead leaves piled at the bottom
of the great gnarled trees with their roots going deep
into the earth. This avenue of trees, reaching high above,
created a canopy which had caught the morning mist,
whose weighted drops dislodged the last of the season's
leaves. ... The Great World Soul is in the golden leaves
falling in season, and for that we give thanks. But when
we plunder Mother Earth, the Great World Soul weeps
through the tears of mothers no longer able to feed their
children. Kill Mother Earth, and we will die.[196]

JOAN WILKINSON
Derbyshire Unitarian

October 25th

Men and boys are learning all kinds of trades – except
how to make *men* of themselves. They learn to make
houses; but they are not so well housed, they are not
so contented in their houses, as the woodchucks in their
holes. What is the use of a house if you haven't got a
tolerable planet to put it on?[197]

HENRY DAVID THOREAU
1817–1862, Transcendentalist poet, philosopher, and naturalist,
raised as a Unitarian

October 26th

Divine Spirit, who calls us to love each other
and to cherish the earth,
we confess our failure to do either very well.
We ask forgiveness for our folly.
Grant us the wit, the wisdom, and the will
to correct it – while there is still time.[198]

CLIFF REED
Unitarian Minister, retired

October 27th

I want to taste and glory in each day, and never be afraid
to experience pain; and never shut myself up in a numb
core of nonfeeling, or stop questioning and criticising life
and take the easy way out. To learn and think; to think
and live; to live and learn: this always, with new insight,
new understanding, and new love.[199]

SYLVIA PLATH
*1932–1963, poet, novelist, member of the Unitarian Universalist Church
in Wellesley, Massachusetts; born on this day*

October 28th

Study the religions of the world, hearken devoutly to
the psalms of the East and to the songs of the West, kneel
silently in the temple of the Buddhist, join in the worship
of the Jewish synagogue, or listen to the prayers of the
Christian Church; in its essence all worship is one, for
all religion is one; for all religion leads to God.[200]

GERTRUD VON PETZOLD
1876–1952, Unitarian, England's first woman minister in any denomination

October 29th

Becoming united with God – however conceived – is what
religion is about, and prayer is the means of enabling
contact to be made. The language of prayer, whether or
not directed to a personal deity, is not important. There is
something about the act of prayer itself which seems to
act as a switch to establish contact with the power that we
call God. Through real prayer, a vast energy is generated
which transforms, enriches, and illuminates, for through
it we are linking ourselves with that Power which is the
inexhaustible motive force which spins the universe.[201]

JOHN ANDREW STOREY
1935–1997, Unitarian minister

October 30th

May we as religious liberals find ways to make connections between justice and love, honouring those who fought for our flourishing and who decorated their banners with garlands. May we live between old stories and new, in peace and joy, borne into the future by the loving hands of those who went before us, who struggled to make our world new and who are always with us, this day, in this world and for all time.

CLAIRE MACDONALD
Unitarian Minister

October 31st
Samhain*

Most years on this day, I take my grandmother's teapot down from a shelf and spend some moments in reflection. She would sit at the table each afternoon for her cup of tea. I can see her sitting there, enjoying this ritual afternoon break. ... Turning the little teapot over in my hands, I remember the years of growing up and being there. The smell of apple pies and the big cups and saucers. The hat and coat she wore for going to church and funerals and her polite friends. She wrote letters at this table and smiled mischievously at me when I wanted to look, or asked who they were for. I used to make up

---

* Samhain is the ancient Celtic festival to mark the end of the harvest and to remember the dead; celebrated from sunset on 31 October to sunset on 1 November.

stories about the people in the photographs to make her laugh, and she would say who they really were; but we had never met them. Her death at an old age broke my heart. I gladly took this little teapot in memory of her. On this day of remembering and honouring our ancestors, I feel the loving hands that nursed this grandmother's teapot. May we all cherish our memories and keep them special.

TONY MCNEILE
Unitarian Earth Spirit Network

NOVEMBER

November 1st
All Saints' Day

A day to remember all saints and martyrs. Unitarian martyrs include NORBERT ČAPEK (1870–1942), who preached religious freedom and died in the gas chamber at the concentration camp in Dachau. His hymns express eternal optimism and hope in the face of death:

> Life is yours, in you I prosper,
> Seed will come to fruit, I know.
> Trust that after winter's snowfall
> Walls will melt and truth will flow.

November 2nd
All Souls' Day

As we slowly tread towards winter,
let us learn how to befriend darkness.
May we find our way in the night and welcome
   the shapes we see.
Let us honour the voices of our ancestors,
and the faces of friends lost through death or conflict.
May we hear their whispers of wisdom,
of laughter and of love.
May their courage to live life fully
provide energy for our dance on the edge of fear.[202]

JOHN HARLEY
Unitarian minister

November 3rd

Happiness is the only good. The time to be happy is
now. The place to be happy is here. The way to be happy
is to make others so. This creed is somewhat short, but
it is long enough for this life; long enough for this world.
If there is another world, when we get there we can
make another creed. But this creed will certainly do
for this life.[203]

ROBERT INGERSOLL
1833–1899, American political leader and orator, a Unitarian agnostic

November 4th

The Dunbar Scot, John Muir (1838–1914), regarded Nature
not merely as a storehouse of raw materials for economic
exploitation, but as a spiritual resource as well. He took a
holistic view of ecology. Human beings were not above
Nature, but themselves part of Nature. Thus he argued
that the preservation of wild places was essential for
reasons of mental health.

Solitude and silence can change the human stance.
Moreover, the presence of noble, beautiful, permanent,
and sublime material forms, accompanied by the gentler
allurements of pure air, fresh flowers, clear streams, and
so on, are precious to us. We are reminded that we are
not of ourselves sufficient unto ourselves.[204]

JOHN MCLACHLAN
1908–2007, Unitarian minister; President of the General Assembly, 1971/72

November 5th

All religions share a common root, which is limitless
compassion. They emphasize human improvement, love,
respect for others and compassion for the suffering of
others. In so far as love is essential in every religion, we
could say that love is a Universal Religion. But the various
techniques and methods for developing love differ widely
between the traditions. I don't think that there could ever
be just one single philosophy or one single religion. Since
there are so many different types of people, with a range
of tendencies and inclinations, it is quite fitting that there

are differences between religions. And the fact that there are so many different descriptions of the religious path shows how rich religion is.

TENZIN GYATSO

The fourteenth – and current – Dalai Lama

November 6th

O Great Spirit, whose voice I hear in the winds,
and whose breath gives life to all the world – hear me.
I am small and weak. I need your strength and wisdom.
Let me walk in beauty, and make my eyes ever behold
the red and purple sunset. Let me learn the lesson
hidden in every leaf and rock.

'RED CLOUD' (MAHPIUA LUTA)

1822–1909, chief of the Native American Oglala Lakota nation

November 7th

As long as coal miners die young and in agony so that
we can have cheap electricity; so long as farm workers
and their children become desperately ill (with no access
to health care) because of exposure to deadly chemicals
that help make our food cheaper; as long as workers
at our favorite "big box" store can be forced to work
overtime without pay and to skip lunch breaks so that we
can consume cheap consumer goods, goods which are
manufactured by people whose working conditions are

even more horrible – we are complicit, whether actively or passively. As Abraham Heschel, the great Jewish thinker and scholar, observed, we live in a world where "few are guilty, but all are responsible." ... I am not free until you are free; and an injury to one really is an injury to all. This is what "community" really means.[205]

AARON B. MCEMRYS

Unitarian Universalist minister, Arlington, Virginia

November 8th

A Unitarian holds the view that no-one has yet found the final and complete truth. We can, however, try to grasp a good measure of it and hold it till we become capable of something more. The search for truth has its own reward – it brings new meaning and dignity into man's life.

GÁBOR KEREKI

1914–1995, Transylvanian Unitarian minister at Croydon
from 1961 until 1984

November 9th

Everything has its season.
All is change and decay:
In each blossom
is contained the russet browns
foretelling the year's end. …

Take each day, each hour, each second,
the only certainty change
and within each dying minute
our reverent acceptance of
the harbingers of renewal.[206]

RICHARD BOBER
Leader of the Unitarian Meditation Fellowship

November 10th

I cannot and will not recant anything, for to go against conscience is neither right nor safe. Here I stand, I can do no other, so help me God. Amen.

MARTIN LUTHER
1483–1546, born on this day

November 11th
Remembrance Day

Comrade, I did not want to kill you ... But you were
only an idea to me before; an abstraction that lived in
my mind and called forth an appropriate response.
It was that abstraction that I stabbed. But now, for the
first time, I see you are a man like me. I thought of your
hand-grenades, of your bayonets, of your rifle; now I
see your wife and your face and our fellowship. Forgive
me, comrade ... If we threw away those rifles and this
uniform, you could be my brother.[207]

ERICH MARIA REMARQUE
1898–1970, German novelist

November 12th

The heavens declare the glory of God, and the firmament
reveals his handiwork. One day speaks to another; and
night with night shares its knowledge, and this without
speech or language, or sound of any voice. Their music
goes out through all the earth, and their words unto the
ends of the world.

PSALM 19: 1−4

November 13th

We pray for wisdom not to be embittered by loss, not
to be made hopeless by frustration, nor withdrawn and
lonely in our sorrow, but to be more out-going, more
heedful, more active and loving through all our days.
May our lives be enriched by the fleeting joys, the
momentary glimpses of beauty, the things of the moment
and of the hour which we may treasure, and weave
into a richer tapestry of memories and meanings.[208]

JACOB TRAPP
1899–1992, Unitarian Universalist minister

November 14th

One of the greatest pleasures of gardening lies in looking
forward. This should make October and November
particularly pleasant months, for then we may begin to
clear our borders, to cut down those sodden and untidy
stalks, to dig up and increase our plants, and to move
them to other positions where they will show up to
greater effect. People who are not gardeners always say
that the bare beds of winter are uninteresting; gardeners
know better, and take even a certain pleasure in the
neatness of the newly dug, bare, brown earth.

VITA SACKVILLE-WEST
1892–1962, poet, novelist and garden designer

November 15th

There are only two ways to live your life. One is as though nothing is a miracle. The other is as though everything is a miracle.

ALBERT EINSTEIN
1879–1955, theoretical physicist

November 16th

Like tides on a crescent sea-beach,
When the moon is new and thin,
Into our hearts high yearnings
Come welling, surging in,
Come from the mystic ocean
Whose rim no foot has trod –
Some people call it longing,
And others call it God.

A picket frozen on duty,
A mother starved for her brood,
And Socrates drinking hemlock,
And Jesus on the rood;
And millions, who, though nameless,
The straight, hard pathway trod –
Some call it consecration,
And others call it God.[209]

WILLIAM HERBERT CARRUTH
1859–1924, American linguist and poet

November 17th

The first Unitarian service that I ever attended included the hymn "Others Call it God" by William Herbert Carruth. [*The text for November 16th.*] But I was quite unable to sing it. The idea that God might be encountered in the "high yearnings" of our hearts, in "a picket frozen on duty" or "a mother starved for her brood" literally took my breath away and filled my eyes with tears. ... The words spoke to me of a divine power that finds expression through each one of us when we dare to live fully and fearlessly from the depths of our hearts and souls; when we willingly make sacrifices out of love and concern for others; and when we allow ourselves to be guided by spirit rather than merely by ego – in other words, when we live with integrity.[210]

KATE WHYMAN
Unitarian minister, Plymouth

November 18th

And if you would know God, be not a solver of riddles. Rather, look about you and you shall see Him playing with your children. And look into space: you shall see Him walking in the cloud, outstretching His arms in the lightning and descending in the rain. You shall see Him smiling in flowers, then rising and waving His hands in trees.[211]

KAHLIL GIBRAN
1883–1931, Lebanese-American writer and artist

November 19th

The most beautiful and most profound experience is the
sensation of the mystical. It is the sower of all true science.
He to whom this emotion is a stranger, who can no longer
wonder and stand rapt in awe, is as good as dead. To know
that what is impenetrable to us really exists, manifesting
itself as the highest wisdom and the most radiant beauty
which our dull faculties can comprehend only in their
primitive forms – this knowledge, this feeling is at the
centre of true religiousness. [212]

ALBERT EINSTEIN
1879–1955, theoretical physicist

November 20th
Universal Children's Day

The great end in religious instruction is not to stamp
our minds irresistibly on the young, but to stir up their
own; not to make them see with our eyes, but to look
inquiringly and steadily with their own; not to give
them a definite amount of knowledge, but to inspire a
fervent love of truth … not to bind them by ineradicable
prejudices to our particular sect or peculiar notions, but
to prepare them for impartial, conscientious judging of
whatever subjects may be offered to their decision …
In a word, the great end is to awaken the soul, to excite
and cherish spiritual life.

WILLIAM ELLERY CHANNING
1780–1842, Unitarian minister and theologian, England and America

November 21st

God gave us the gift of life; it is up to us to give ourselves
the gift of living well.

VOLTAIRE

1694–1778, French Enlightenment philosopher, born on this day

November 22nd

A Song for St Cecilia's Day, 1687

From harmony, from heavenly harmony,
This universal frame began:
When nature underneath a heap
Of jarring atoms lay,
And could not heave her head,
The tuneful voice was heard from high,
'Arise, ye more than dead!'
Then cold, and hot, and moist, and dry,
In order to their stations leap,
And Music's power obey.
From harmony, from heavenly harmony,
This universal frame began:
From harmony to harmony
Through all the compass of the notes it ran,
The diapason closing full in Man.

JOHN DRYDEN

1631–1700, English poet

November 23rd

As a single footstep will not make a path on the earth,
so a single thought will not make a pathway in the mind.
To make a deep physical path, we walk again and again.
To make a deep mental path, we must think over and
over the kind of thoughts we wish to dominate our lives.

HENRY DAVID THOREAU
1817–1862, Transcendentalist poet, philosopher, and naturalist,
raised as a Unitarian

November 24th

Earth teach me caring – as mothers nurture their young.
Earth teach me courage – as the tree that stands alone.
Earth teach me limitation – as the ant that crawls on
   the ground.
Earth teach me freedom – as the eagle that soars in the sky.
Earth teach me acceptance – as the leaves that die each fall.
Earth teach me renewal – as the seed that rises in the spring.
Earth teach me to forget myself – as melted snow forgets
   its shape.

From A PRAYER OF THE UTE PEOPLE
after whom the state of Utah is named

November 25th

My church values people, change and experiment …
being different. Seeks insights in poetry and music,
and the prophets of all faiths. And in silence … deep,
creative silence. I do not worship, but am in awe of
the mysterious, I experience and grow. My church is
everywhere – mountain top and city square, Inside,
outside … no barriers.

ANONYMOUS

November 26th

O Holy One, we thank you for human love, where,
in true caring for another, the divine shines through the
human … we thank you for love's power to transfigure
and to heal … for life's enrichment in work well done
for love's sake … for beauty, wherein we may see and
feel your radiance within and around us. Give us to seek
and to find everywhere and in all things the beauty of
your presence.[213]

BRUCE FINDLOW
Unitarian minister, Principal of Manchester College Oxford 1974–1985

November 27th

An eye for an eye only ends up making the whole world blind.

The best way to find yourself is to lose yourself in the service of others.

MAHATMA GANDHI

1869–1948

November 28th

In this town I pursued for a time my studies of theology. I had no professor or teacher to guide me; but I had two noble places of study. One was yonder beautiful edifice, now frequented and useful as a public library, then so deserted that I spent day after day, and sometimes week after week, amidst its dusty volumes, without interruption from a single visitor.

The other place was yonder beach, the roar of which has so often mingled with the worship of this place, my daily resort, dear to me in the sunshine, still more attractive in the storm. Seldom do I visit now without thinking of the work which there, in the sight of that beauty, in the sound of those waves, was carried on in my soul.[214]

WILLIAM ELLERY CHANNING

1780–1842, Unitarian minister and theologian, England and America

November 29th

We are all living and dying. I do not know when my death will come, and because I embrace the not-knowing, I take it as my responsibility to prepare myself. Just as I accepted the precious gift of life in me, so I will accept my death. It may not be easy: some deaths are hard. But, however it will be for me, I choose to be open to the mystery of it. I want to prepare for death, not in the sense of trying to be in control, but in the sense of being ready to live my dying, opening to a vast unknown.[215]

ELIZABETH BIRTLES
Unitarian minister, retired

November 30th

St Andrew's Day

O, wad some Power the giftie gie us
To see oursels as others see us!
It wad frae monie a blunder free us,
An' foolish notion.[216]

ROBERT BURNS
1759–1796, Scotland's national poet; a Unitarian sympathiser

DECEMBER

December 1st

Compassion, then, before anything else, is the work of feeling with the other. And it *is* work – ask any therapist – emotional work, psychic work, spiritual work; we might call it heart work, womb work, gut work. It is work which demands the focusing of attention on the other and thus requires a radical de-centring of the ego; work which often requires a patience and endurance in the presence of the other's intractable reality. Being with the other in all the different moods of their passion is a costly process.[217]

NICOLA SLEE
Feminist poet and theologian

December 2nd

Each of us, from birth to death, is vulnerable to the ebbs
and flows of life: the natural transitions, the randomness,
the consequences of our own and others' choices.
Paying attention to the moments of our lives is a spiritual
practice best done in the context of a caring, affirming
community. To live an ethic of care calls us not to act
carelessly, nor to abandon one another. It takes a village
to sustain a soul.[218]

JILL JARVIS
Unitarian Universalist minister

December 3rd

I say religion isn't about believing things. It's ethical
alchemy. It's about behaving in a way that changes you,
that gives you intimations of holiness and sacredness.[219]

KAREN ARMSTRONG
Writer, theologian and founder of the Charter for Compassion

December 4th

At the heart of a progressive Muslim interpretation is
a simple yet radical idea: every human life, female and
male, Muslim and non-Muslim, rich or poor, "Northern"
or "Southern", has exactly the same intrinsic worth.
The essential value of human life is God-given, and is

in no way connected to culture, geography, or privilege. A progressive Muslim is one who is committed to the strangely controversial idea that the worth of a human being is measured by a person's character, not the oil under their soil, and not their flag. A progressive Muslim agenda is concerned with the ramifications of the premise that all members of humanity have this same intrinsic worth because, as the Qur'an reminds us, each of us has the breath of God breathed into our being.[220]

OMID SAFI
Professor of Asian and Middle Eastern Studies, Duke University

December 5th

As I walk, as I walk,
the universe is walking with me:
in beauty it walks before me,
in beauty it walks behind me,
in beauty it walks below me,
in beauty it walks above me.
Beauty is on every side.
As I walk, I walk with beauty.

A PRAYER OF THE NAVAJO PEOPLE
IN THE AMERICAN SOUTH-WEST

December 6th

Everybody loves progress, but nobody likes change.

ANONYMOUS

We should like to have some towering geniuses, to reveal us to ourselves in colour and fire, but of course they would have to fit into the pattern of our society and be able to take orders from sound administrative types.

J. B. PRIESTLEY
1894–1984, novelist and playwright

December 7th

Celebration is an active state, an act of expressing reverence or appreciation. To be entertained is a passive state – it is to receive pleasure afforded by an amusing act or a spectacle. Entertainment is a diversion, a distraction of the mind from the preoccupations of daily living. Celebration is a confrontation, giving attention to the transcendent meaning of one's actions. Celebration is an act of expressing respect or reverence for that which one needs or honours. In modern usage, the term suggests demonstrations, often public demonstrations, of joy and festivity, such as singing, shouting, speechmaking, feasting, and the like. Yet what I mean is not outward ceremony and public demonstration, but rather inward appreciation, lending spiritual form to everyday

acts. Its essence is to call attention to the sublime or
solemn aspects of living, to rise above the confines of
consumption.[221]

ABRAHAM JOSHUA HESCHEL
1907–1972, Polish-born American rabbi, theologian, and philosopher

December 8th

The beautiful souls are they that are universal, open, and
ready for all things.

MICHEL DE MONTAIGNE
1533–1592, philosopher and essayist

December 9th

A journey can become a sacred thing:
Make sure, before you go,
To take the time
To bless your going forth,
To free your heart of ballast
So that the compass of your soul
Might direct you toward
The territories of spirit
Where you will discover
More of your hidden life,
And the urgencies
That deserve to claim you.[222]

JOHN O'DONOHUE
1956–2008, poet, author, priest and philosopher

December 10th

Margaret the Churchwoman, her father the Dissenter, and Higgins the Infidel knelt down together. It did them no harm.[223]

ELIZABETH GASKELL
Unitarian novelist, 1810–1865

December 11th

We can come to know the world as paradise when our hearts and souls are reborn through the arduous and tender task of living rightly with one another and the earth. Generosity, nonviolence, and care for one another are the pathways into transformed awareness. Knowing that paradise is here and now is a gift that comes to those who practice the ethics of paradise. This way of living is not Utopian. It does not spring simply from the imagination of a better world, but from a profound embrace of this world. It does not begin with knowledge or hope. It begins with love.[224]

RITA NAKASHIMI BROCK and REBECCA ANN PARKER
Feminist theologians, activists and educators

December 12th

We are not going to be able to operate our Spaceship
Earth successfully nor for much longer unless we see it
as a whole spaceship and our fate as common. It has to
be everybody or nobody.[225]

R. BUCKMINSTER FULLER
1895–1983, Unitarian Universalist, architect, systems theorist

December 13th

The pursuit of happiness is more elusive; it is lifelong,
and it is not goal-centred. What you are pursuing is
meaning – a meaningful life. There's the hap – the fate,
the draw that is yours, and it isn't fixed; but changing
the course of the stream, or dealing new cards, whatever
metaphor you want to use – that's going to take a lot of
energy. There are times when it will go so wrong that you
will barely be alive, and times when you realize that being
barely alive, on your own terms, is better than living
a bloated half-life on someone else's terms.[226]

JEANETTE WINTERSON
Writer, broadcaster, and professor of creative writing

December 14th

The world you see is just a movie in your mind.
Rocks don't see it.
Bless and sit down.
Forgive and forget.
Practice kindness all day to everybody
and you will realize you're already
in heaven now.
That's the story.
That's the message.[227]

JACK KEROUAC
1922–1969, novelist and poet

December 15th

We pause in reverence before the mystery of a presence
in whom we live and move and have our being, wherein,
although we are separate, we are together, wherein,
although we are many, we are one.[228]

JACOB TRAPP
1899–1992, Unitarian Universalist minister

December 16th

The truth is this: If there is no justice, there will be no peace. We can read Thoreau and Emerson to one another, quote Rilke and Alice Walker and Howard Thurman, and think good and noble thoughts about ourselves. But if we cannot bring justice into the small circle of our own individual lives, we cannot hope to bring justice to the world. And if we do not bring justice to the world, none of us is safe and none of us will survive. Nothing that Unitarian Universalists need to do is more important than making justice real – here, where we are. Hard as diversity is, it is our most important task.[229]

ROSEMARY BRAY MCNATT
Unitarian Universalist minister, President of the
Starr King School for the Ministry

December 17th

O God, when we want to do only what costs us nothing, show us how great a cost it is when the nothingness of what we do comes back, and nothingness is all we have within us.[230]

A. POWELL DAVIES
1902–1957, Unitarian minister

December 18th

Thinking about the things that I do associate with the
full sort of happiness that really reaches through me,
I've realised I am happier the more that I am being
myself. Not the version of myself that I *think* people
want to see, or expect to see, but when the outside of
me truly resonates with the inside of me. Expressing
that version of myself, and connecting with other
people who recognise and understand it, brings an easy
flowing happiness that I'd choose every time over a fancy
restaurant. And I've realised that part of expressing that
version of me in the world is accepting it myself – that
self-acceptance feels much more than a cause of being
happy, but part of being happy in itself.[231]

ELIZABETH SLADE
Chief Officer, General Assembly of Unitarian and Free Christian Churches

December 19th

Time is the heartbeat of existence: this moment here,
when grace breaks through the meaninglessness of
objects in space. Meaning breaks through our busyness
and stops us in our tracks. With a simple turning, we are
met with divinity.[232]

NANCY JAY CRUMBINE
Writer, activist and Unitarian Universalist minister

December 20th

All of us have monarchs and sages for kinsmen; nay,
angels and archangels for cousins; since in antediluvian
days, the sons of God did verily wed with our mothers,
the irresistible daughters of Eve. Thus all generations
are blended: and heaven and earth of one kin: the
hierarchies of seraphs in the uttermost skies; the thrones
and principalities in the zodiac; the shades that roam
throughout space; the nations and families, flocks and folds
of the earth; one and all, brothers in essence – oh, be we
then brothers indeed! All things form but one whole.[233]

HERMAN MELVILLE
1819–1891, Unitarian author of Moby Dick

December 21st

Lo for the tiding of the long night moon
Let the sunrise call about the morning soon
Short is the biding of the fading light
Sing for the coming of the longest night.

North wind tell us what we need to know
When the stars are shining on the midnight snow
All of the branches will be turned to white
Sing for the coming of the longest night.[234]

IAIN FRISK
Songwriter, composer

December 22nd

Ancient practices have commonalities and specificities.
Old ways often require to be renewed, even to die and be
reborn. My own desire is to allow the echoes of ancient
voices and stories to come through to us – because
they continue to inform us. They can operate to enable
sharing, and they work with the most ancient of symbols
and materials – water, bread, tables, earth, fire, telling
stories to keep away the dark, and to make ourselves
safe in community. They allow us to be present to one
another, to mark the passing of the days, and to mark
the shared passing of time.

CLAIRE MACDONALD
Minister, Lewisham Unitarians

December 23rd

He that lives in Love lives in God, says the Beloved
Disciple: And to be sure, a Man can live nowhere
better. ... Love is above all; and when it prevails in us
all, we shall all be Lovely, and in Love with God and
one with another.[235]

WILLIAM PENN
1644–1718, Quaker founder of the State of Pennsylvania

December 24th

For so the children come, and so they have been coming.

Always the same way they come, born of the seed of a man and a woman.

No angels herald their beginnings. No prophets predict their future courses.

No wise men see a star to show where to find the babe that will save humankind.

Yet each night a child is born is a holy night.

Sitting beside our children's cribs, we feel glory in the sight of new life beginning.

We ask "Where and how will this new life end? Or will it ever end?"

Each night a child is born is a holy night.

A time for singing, a time for wondering, a time for worshiping.

SOPHIA LYON FAHS
1876–1978, Unitarian Universalist author and teacher

December 25th

I know what I really want for Christmas. I want my childhood back. Nobody is going to give me that. I might give at least the memory of it to myself if I try. I know it doesn't make sense, but since when is Christmas about sense, anyway? It is about a child, of long ago and far away, and it is about the child of now. In you and me. Waiting behind the door of our hearts for something wonderful to happen. A child who is impractical, unrealistic, simpleminded and terribly vulnerable to joy.[236]

ROBERT FULGHUM
*Minister Emeritus, Unitarian Universalist Church,
Edmonds, Washington DC*

December 26th

Let no ungenerous thought be in our minds today, no intent that is hurtful to another, no purpose that has harm in it. Touch us, O God, with the sweet simplicity of Christmas joy, and may its gentleness and lovingkindness fill our hearts.[237]

A. POWELL DAVIES
1902–1957, Unitarian minister

December 27th

Living lives of greater integrity? Is it perhaps something to do with quite simply reminding ourselves of the power of human kindness, kindness for ourselves, and for others? Maybe it comes down to allowing the power of love to flow through us, seeking and understanding the blockages to the flow of love in us and in others. Maybe it comes down to offering a helping hand to those we find trapped, stuck or lost along the way. One day, maybe, a similar hand will reach out to us when we need it most.[238]

SARAH TINKER
Minister of the Essex Church Unitarian congregation in Kensington

December 28th

Hope is the thing with feathers
That perches in the soul,
And sings the tune without the words,
And never stops at all.

And sweetest in the gale is heard
And sore must be the storm
That could abash the little bird
That kept so many warm.[239]

EMILY DICKINSON
1830–1836, Massachusetts poet

December 29th

The path of awakening and loving is a path without
end. We cannot measure the worth of a single loving
action, or the impact of a single caring gesture. We cannot
know the results of a single meditation, or evaluate the
learning we will derive by meeting a single difficulty with
open-heartedness. When we connect with the precious
richness of loving, caring, and connectedness, results fade
in importance. We can only trust that the landscape
we paint will be colored by our love and care.[240]

JOHN KORNFIELD and CHRISTINA FELDMAN

December 30th

When the song of the angels is stilled,
when the star in the sky is gone,
when the kings and princes are home,
when the shepherds are back with their flocks,
the work of Christmas begins:
to find the lost,
to heal the broken,
to feed the hungry,
to release the prisoner,
to rebuild the nations,
to bring peace among the people,
to make music in the heart.[241]

HOWARD THURMAN
1899–1981, African-American philosopher and civil-rights leader

December 31st

My last word has to be *gratitude*, gratitude for being
… It shows ingratitude and a lack of imagination to
spend the life we have been given stamping literally
or metaphorically on the lives of others or sneering
contemptuously at how they have chosen to make sense
of theirs. It is a harsh world, indescribably cruel. It is a
gentle world, unbelievably beautiful. It is a world that
can make us bitter, hateful, rabid destroyers of joy. It is a
world that can draw forth tenderness from us, as we lean
towards one another over broken gates. It is a world of
monsters and saints, a mutilated world, but it is the only
one we have been given. We should let it shock us not
into hate or anxiety, but into unconditional love.[242]

RICHARD HOLLOWAY
Writer, broadcaster and former Bishop of Edinburgh

SOURCES

1 Ford, James Ishmael: extract from *Already Broken: A Buddhist Perspective on the Season of Spring* (www.uua.org/worship/words/sermon/19845. shtml).

2 Short, Harry Lismer: *Divine Discontent* (Cambridge & Montmorrat: Sebastien Castellio Press, 2010).

3 Reed, Cliff: *Carnival of Lamps* (London: The Lindsey Press, 2014).

4 Emerson, Dorothy May: www.uua.org/worship/words/meditation/5823.shtml.

5 Burroughs, John: *Accepting the Universe: Essays in Naturalism* (1920).

6 Storey, John Andrew: 'Benediction' in *Reflections: An Anthology of Prayers, Meditations, and Poems by Contemporary Unitarians* (London: Unitarian Worship Sub-Committee, 1979).

7 Tarbox, Elizabeth: *Evening Tide* (Boston, MA: Skinner House Books, 1998; available from www.uua.org/bookstore).

8 Chesterton, G.K.: from an early notebook (mid-1890s).

9 Davis, A. Powell: 'Where Now is Thy God?': a sermon preached on 8 December 1946 (http://dmuuc.org/aboutworship/dr-a-powell-davies-bio-sermons/where-thy-god/).

10 Schweitzer, Albert: 'The ethic of reverence for life', in *Civilization and Ethics*, ed. C.T. Campion (London: Adam & Charles Black, 1967).

11 King, Martin Luther Jr: *Letter from the Birmingham Jail* (New York City: HarperOne, 1994).

12 Robinson, Jonathan: *The Grail Liturgies: An Alternative Form for the Eucharist and Morning and Evening Prayer.*

13 Mandela, Nelson: *Long Walk to Freedom: The Autobiography of Nelson Mandela* (Boston, MA: Little Brown & Co., 1995).

14 Findlow, Bruce: 'A Liturgy' (c. 1975).

15 Usher, David: *Twelve Steps to Spiritual Health* (London: The Lindsey Press, 2013).

16 Marcus Aurelius, *Meditations,* Book Two (167 CE).

17 Smith, Matthew: unpublished sermon.

18 Levi, Primo: interview in *The New Republic,* 17 February 1986.

19 Darlison, Bill: 'Don't Nobody Know Why', in *With Heart and Mind,* ed. David Dawson (London: The Worship Panel of the General Assembly of Unitarian and Free Christian Churches, 2007).

20 Elworthy, Scilla: from an address given to the Oxford Unitarian congregation in February 2004.

21 Trapp, Jacob: *Intimations of Grandeur: Meditations by Jacob Trapp* (London: The Lindsey Press, 1968).

22 Tutu, Desmond M. and Mpho Tutu: *The Book of Forgiving: The Four-fold Path for Healing Ourselves and Our World* (Harper Collins, 2014).

23 Parks, Rosa: *My Story* (New York: Dial Books, 1992).

24 Howe, Anthony: 'The Sacred in the Everyday', www.unitarian.org.uk/pages/meditations-and-reflections.

25 Dickens, Charles: *Great Expectations* (1860).

26 Paine, Thomas: *Rights of Man* (1791).

27 Lamb, Charles: *Essays of Elia* (1823).

28 Quoted by Hillary Rodham Clinton in her book *Living History* (New York: Scribner, 2003).

29 Guengerich, Galen: *God Revised: How Religion Must Evolve in a Scientific Age* (Palgrave Macmillan, 2013).

30 Penn, William: *Some Fruits of Solitude in Reflections and Maxims* (1682).

31 York, Sarah: 'Mutual Love' from *Into the Wilderness* (Apollo Ranch Institute Press, 2000).

32 Anthony, Susan B: quoted in *The Ghost in My Life* by her great-niece of the same name (Chosen Books, 1971).

33 Reed, Cliff: 'We Give Thanks', *We Are Here: A Book of Prayers for Corporate Worship* (London: The Lindsey Press, 1992).

34 Monk, David: 'Time and Eternity', *With Heart and Mind,* ed. David Dawson (London: The Worship Panel of the General Assembly of Unitarian and Free Christian Churches, 2007).

35 Parker, Theodore: quoted by William J. Doherty, 'Time to commit', *UU World*, January/February 2005 (www.uuworld.org/2005/01/feature3.html).

36 Storey, John Andrew: *The Common Quest,* eds. Charles Hughes and Sylvia Storey (London: The Lindsey Press, 2000).

37 Howe, Anthony: 'The Sacred in the Everyday', www.unitarian.org.uk/pages/meditations-and-reflections.

38 Thursfield, Alison: 'Snakes and Ladders', *With Heart and Mind,* ed. David Dawson (London: The Worship Panel of the General Assembly of Unitarian and Free Christian Churches, 2007).

39 Trapp, Jacob: *Intimations of Grandeur: Meditations by Jacob Trapp* (London: The Lindsey Press, 1968).

40 Usher, David: extract from a comment piece published in *The Church Times* following Chester Cathedral's refusal to host a Unitarian service, 2006.

41 Davies, A. Powell: *The Language of the Heart* (New York: Farrar, Straus, and Cudahy, 1956).

42 Alcott, Louisa May: *Little Women* (1868).

43 Anthony, Susan B.: quoted in *An Account of the Proceedings of the Trial of Susan B. Anthony on the Charge of Illegal Voting* (1874).

44 Traherne, Thomas: *Centuries of Meditations. The Third Century* (London: Dobell, 1908).

45 Wollstonecraft, Mary: *Letters Written during a Short Residence in Sweden, Norway and Denmark* (1796).

46 Priestley, Joseph: *Institutes of Natural and Revealed Religion* (1772).

47 Trapp, Jacob: *Intimations of Grandeur: Meditations by Jacob Trapp* (London: The Lindsey Press, 1968).

48 Conway, Verona: 'Prayer', *Reflections: An Anthology of Prayers, Meditations, and Poems by Contemporary Unitarians* (London: Unitarian Worship Subcommittee, 1979).

49 The Hindu Vedas.

50 Keip, Margaret: *Honoring Earth* (www.uua.org/worship/words/opening/25349.shtml).

51 Darlison, Bill: from a sermon, 'The Many-Splendoured Thing', reprinted in *The Unitarian Life: Voices from the Past and Present*, ed. Stephen Lingwood (London: The General Assembly of Unitarian and Free Christian Churches).

52 Hodges, Steve: from an address entitled 'Matters of Life and Death', given at a Unitarian service in Oxford in December 2016.

53 Schweitzer, Albert: *Albert Schweitzer: An Anthology* (Beacon Press, 1947).

54 Reed, Cliff: 'Remind Us', in *Reflections: An Anthology of Prayers, Meditations, and Poems by Contemporary Unitarians* (London: Unitarian Worship Sub-Committee, 1979).

55 Spong, John Shelby: *Eternal Life: A New Vision* (HarperCollins, 2009).

56 Dawson, David: 'Celebrating the Arts', *Marking the Days. A Book of Occasional Services* (London: The Lindsey Press, 2006).

57 Lingwood, Stephen: *The Inquirer,* March 2009.

58 www.uua.org/worship/words/chalice-lighting/let-there-be-light-0.

59 Johnson, Penny: 'Clutter', *With Heart and Mind*, ed. David Dawson (London: The Worship Panel of the General Assembly of Unitarian and Free Christian Churches, 2007).

60 Schweitzer, Albert: *Kulturphilosophie, Vol. 2: Civilization and Ethics* (1923).

61 Channing, William Ellery: *The Perfect Life: In Twelve Discourses* (1841).

62 Dadson, Michael: 'Let It Show', *With Heart and Mind,* ed. David Dawson (London: The Worship Panel of the General Assembly of Unitarian and Free Christian Churches, 2007).

63 Hazlitt, William: *Edinburgh Review* (October 1829).

64 Barton, Clara: *The Story of My Childhood* (1907), https://archive.org/details/storymychildhoooobartgoog

65 Jefferson, Thomas: The American Declaration of Independence, 1776.

66 Smart, Christopher: 'For I will consider my Cat Jeoffry', from Fragment B of *Jubilate Agno*.

67 Wittenburg, Jonathan: 'My Dog is Arguably a Better Spiritual Guide Than Me', *The Times* 27 October 2018.

68 King, Martin Luther Jr: 'Loving your Enemies', a sermon preached at Christmas 1957 in the Dexter Avenue Baptist Church, Montgomery, Alabama.

69 Walker, Frank: 'Spring and Words', *Celebrating Easter and Spring: An Anthology of Unitarian Universalist Readings* compiled by Carl Seaburg and Mark Harris (Cambridge, MA: The Anne Miniver Press, 2000).

70 McCready, Tom: 'A Celtic Service for Bloomsday', *Marking the Days: A Book of Occasional Services* (London: The Lindsey Press, 2006).

71 Martineau, James: from a speech at the opening of Manchester College in Oxford in 1893.

72 Dostoyevsky, Fyodor: *The Brothers Karamazov* (1879).

73 Davies, A. Powell: *The Language of the Heart* (New York: Farrar, Straus and Cudahy, 1956).

74 Short, Harry Lismer: *Divine Discontent* (Cambridge & Montmorrat: Sebastien Castellio Press, 2010).

75 Usher, David: *Twelve Steps to Spiritual Health* (London: The Lindsey Press, 2013).

76 Emerson, Ralph Waldo: *Nature* (1836).

77 Toye, John: from a sermon preached for Oxford Unitarians in 2012.

78 Bowes, Jeffrey: 'Workers' Memorial Day', *Marking the Days: A Book of Occasional Services,* ed. Kate Taylor (London: The Lindsey Press, 2006).

79 Seeger, Pete, interviewed in *New York Times Magazine*, 22 January 1995.

80 Monk, David: 'Time and Eternity', *With Heart and Mind*, ed. David Dawson (London: The General Assembly of Unitarian and Free Christian Churches, 2007).

81 Gibran, Kahlil: *The Prophet* (London: William Heinemann, 1926).

82 Whitman, Walt: 'Song of the Open Road', *Leaves of Grass* (1856).

83 Diderot, Denis: *Pensées philosophiques* (1746).

84 Reed, Cliff: *Carnival of Lamps* (London: General Assembly of Unitarian and Free Christian Churches, 2015).

85 Nightingale, Florence: *Notes on Nursing: What It Is, and What It Is Not* (1859).

86 Ingersoll, Robert G.: in discussion with Rev. Henry M. Field on Faith and Agnosticism, quoted in Vol. VI of Farrell's edition of his works.

87 Usher, David: *Twelve Steps to Spiritual Health* (London: The Lindsey Press, 2013).

88 Traherne, Thomas: *Centuries of Meditations* (London: Dobell, 1908).

89 Curry, Michael: *The Power of Love* (Hodder & Stoughton, 2018).

90 Quoted in *The Rainbow of Faiths* by John Hick (Westminster: John Knox Press, 1995).

91 Davies, A. Powell: *Without Apology: Collected Meditations on Liberal Religion by A. Powell Davies*, ed. Forrest Church (Boston: Skinner House Books, 1998; available from www.uua/bookstore).

92 Hawkins, Peter: 'Taking Our Values to Work', *Living with Integrity: Unitarian Values and Beliefs in Practice*, ed. Kate Whyman (London: The Lindsey Press, 2016).

93 Seccombe, Josephine: from *Nine Steps to Mentoring with the Enneagram in the Narrative Tradition* (Association of the Enneagram in the Narrative Tradition, 2013).

94 Stevenson, Adlai, quoted in John A. Buehrens and Forrest Church: *A Chosen Faith* (Boston: Beacon Press, 1998).

95 Usher, David: from a sermon preached for Oxford Unitarians in 2009.

96 *The Inquirer* (probably February 2008).

97 Hammarskjöld, Dag: from his private journal, published in 1963 after his death under the title *Markings* (Vintage Books, 2006).

98 Law, William: *A Serious Call to a Devout and Holy Life* (1729).

99 Thoreau, Henry David: diary entry, January 1857.

100 Eliot, George: *Adam Bede* (1859).

101 Naish, John: 'Living Sustainably', *Living with Integrity*, ed. Kate Whyman (London: The Lindsey Press, 2016).

102 Emerson, Ralph Waldo (adapted): 'These Roses', in *Singing the Living Tradition* (Boston: Unitarian Universalist Association, 1993), reading 556.

103 Traherne, Thomas: *Centuries of Meditations* (London: Dobell).

104 Chekov, Anton: *Uncle Vanya* (1898).

105 Mason, Leonard: *Hinge of the Year – Christmas Crosstalk* (London: The Lindsey Press, 1967).

106 Short, Harry Lismer: *Divine Discontent* (Cambridge: Sebastien Castellio Press, 2010).

107 Ruskin, John: *The Stones of Venice* (1851).

108 Larson, Philip: *Tides of Spring* (Boston USA: Unitarian Universalist Association, 1972).

109 Barton, Jane: 'Reflection', *With Heart and Mind,* ed. David Dawson (London, The Worship Panel of the General Assembly of Unitarian and Free Christian Churches, 2007).

110 Lovis, Richard: 'Moorland Matins at Huntingdon Cross', *Celebration* (London: Unitarian Worship Subcommittee, 1988).

111 Thomas, Edward: 'In Memoriam – Easter 1915'.

112 Davies, A. Powell: *The Language of the Heart: A Book of Prayers by A. Powell Davies* (New York: Farrar, Straus and Cudahy, 1956).

113 Brianson, Alex: 'Championing the Environment and Greening the Spirit', *Living with Integrity: Unitarian Values and Beliefs in Practice*, ed. Kate Whyman (London: The Lindsey Press, 2016).

114 Davies, A. Powell: *The Language of the Heart* (New York: Farrar, Straus, and Cudahy, 1956).

115 Whitman, Walt: *Leaves of Grass* (1855).

116 Boeke, Johanna: 'Before the Action, the Pause', *With Heart and Mind*, ed. David Dawson (London, The Worship Panel of the General Assembly of Unitarian and Free Christian Churches, 2007).

117 Tinker, Sarah: *Stirrings* (Unitarian College Manchester, 2004).

118 Trapp, Jacob: *Intimations of Grandeur: Meditations by Jacob Trapp* (London: The Lindsey Press, 1968).

119 Griffiths, Bede: *The Universal Christ* (London: Darton, Longman & Todd, 1990).

120 Walsh, Robert R.: *Stone Blessings* (Boston: Skinner House Books, 2010; available from www.uua/bookstore).

121 von Petzold, Gertrud: sermon entitled 'The Vison of Paul', *The Higher Life* (Manchester, 1908) (www.hibbbert-assembly.org.uk/womenswork).

122 Seng-ts'an: *Hsin Hsin Ming,* CE 606.

123 Dean, Kate: from 'Prayer for All' in *Stirrings 2018,* ed. by Mark Hutchinson (Unitarian College Manchester, 2018).

124 Havel, Václav: *Living in Truth* (Faber and Faber, 1989).

125 Sandburg, Carl: *Incidentals* (1904).

126 Tagore, Rabindranath: *Gitanjali* (Song Offerings) (New York: Macmillan, 1916).

127 Hazlitt, William: 'On Prejudice', *Sketches and Essays* (1839).

128 Tutu, Desmond and Mpho Tutu: *The Book of Forgiving* (London: William Collins, 2015).

129 Seccombe, Josephine: prayer composed for an Oxford Unitarian service in 2012 on the occasion of the departure of a much-loved organist.

130 Davies, A. Powell: *The Language of the Heart* (New York: Farrar, Straus and Cudahy, 1956).

131 Short, Harry Lismer: 'Creativeness', *Echoes: A Second Anthology of Prayers, Meditations, and Poems by Contemporary Unitarians* (London: Unitarian Worship Sub-Committee, 1982).

132 Trapp, Jacob: 'To Worship', *Singing the Living Tradition* (Boston: Unitarian Universalist Association, 1993), reading 441.

133 Rogers, Elizabeth: 'We Can All Try', *Echoes: A Second Anthology of Prayers, Meditations, and Poems by Contemporary Unitarians* (London: Unitarian Worship Sub-Committee, 1982).

134 Clough, Bert: prayer based on an extract from *Under the Sea-Wind* by Rachel Carson (Simon & Schuster, 1941).

135 Short, Harry Lismer: 'Problems and Solutions', *Divine Discontent* (Cambridge: Sebastien Castellio Press, 2010).

136 Bynner, Witter: *The Way of Life According to Lao Tzu* (G P Putnam's Sons, 1949).

137 Donne, John: 'No Man Is An Island', *Meditation* XVII; *Devotions upon Emergent Occasions* (1624).

138 Nightingale, Florence: letter to Benjamin Jowett, 1867.

139 Knight, Sydney H.: *Songs for Living and Words of Worship* (London: The Lindsey Press, 1972).

140 Davies, A. Powell: *The Language of the Heart* (New York: Farrar, Straus and Cudahy, 1956).

141 Findlow, Bruce: 'A Liturgy' (c. 1975).

142 Pauling, Linus: *No More War!* (Dodd, Mead & Co., 1958).

143 Easton, Marjorie: 'Silence', *Reflections: An Anthology of Prayers, Meditations, and Poems by Contemporary Unitarians* (London: Unitarian Worship Sub-Committee, 1979).

144 Beaudreault, Don: 'Angels Among Us', *With Heart and Mind,* ed. David Dawson (London: The General Assembly of Unitarian and Free Christian Churches, 2007).

145 Bradbury, Ray: *Fahrenheit 451* (Ballantine Publishing, 1953).

146 Goudge, Elizabeth: *The Joy of the Snow: An Autobiography* (Hodder and Stoughton, 1974).

147 Keane, Feargal: 'Try To Be Kind', in *You Have Breath for No More than 99 Words: What Would They Be?* (collected by Liz Gray, published by Darton, Longman & Todd, 2011).

148 Rohr, Richard: *Immortal Diamond: The Search for Our True Self* (Jossey-Bass, 2012).

149 McCready, Tom: 'Maundy Thursday Communion', *Marking the Days: A Book of Occasional Services* (London: The Lindsey Press, 2006).

150 Brussatt, Frederic and Mary: *Spiritual Literacy: Reading the Sacred in Everyday Life* (New York: Scribner, 1998).

151 Williamson, Marianne: *A Return To Love: Reflections on the Principles of A Course in Miracles* (Harper Collins, 1992).

152 Trapp, Jacob: *Intimations of Grandeur* (London: Lindsey Press, 1968).

153 Burns, Colleen: *The Inquirer* (date unknown).

154 Lovis, Richard: 'Let Us Be Grateful', *A Fair Field Full of Folk* (London: Unitarian General Assembly Worship Committee, 1997).

155 Davies, A. Powell: *The Language of the Heart* (New York: Farrar, Straus and Cudahy, 1956).

156 Čapek, Norbert, quoted in *Norbert Čapek: Spiritual Journey* by Richard Henry (Skinner House Books, 1999; available from www.uua/bookstore).

157 Obama, Barack: interviewed in *The New Yorker* in 2016.

158 Blake, William: 'On Another's Sorrow', *Songs of Innocence and Experience* (1789).

159 Gibran, Kahlil: *The Prophet* (London: William Heinemann, 1926).

160 Weil, Simone: *Waiting for God* (Putnam, 1951).

161 Schweitzer, Albert; quoted in *Reverence for Life: Albert Schweitzer's Great Contribution to Ethical Thought* by Ara Paul Barsam (New York: Oxford University Press, 2008).

162 Davies, A. Powell: *The Language of the Heart* (New York: Farrar, Straus and Cudahy, 1956).

163 Einstein, Albert, quoted in *The Quantum and the Lotus: A Journey to the Frontiers Where Science and Buddhism Meet*, by Matthieu Ricard and Trinh Thuan (Broadway Books, 2004).

164 Eliot, George: *Adam Bede* (1859).

165 Wilkins, Howard: 'A Remembrance Day Service', *Marking the Days: A Collection of Services for Special Occasions for Use in the Unitarian and Free Christian Tradition,* ed. Kate Taylor (London: The Lindsey Press, 2006).

166 Curtis, Maria: 'Divine Spirit of Compassion', *Poverty in our Midst: 'The Poor Shall Inherit?'* (Stirrings 2014, Unitarian College Manchester).

167 Usher, David: 'A Service for Prison Sunday', *Marking the Days: A Collection of Services for Special Occasions for Use in the Unitarian and Free Christian Tradition,* ed. Kate Taylor (London: The Lindsey Press, 2006).

168 Gaskell, Elizabeth: *North and South* (1855).

169 Walker, Frank: 'Harvest Prayer', *Celebration: Another Anthology of Prayers, Meditations, and Poems by Contemporary Unitarians* (London: Unitarian Worship Subcommittee, 1998).

170 Bynner, Witter: *The Way of Life According to Lao Tzu* (G P Putnam's Sons, 1949).

171 Underhill, Evelyn: *The Life of the Spirit and the Life of Today* (London: Methuen, 1922).

172 Channing, William Ellery: *Spiritual Freedom* (1830).

173 Walsh, Robert R.: www.uua.org/worship/words/reading/more-we-deserve (Unitarian Universalist Association).

174 Main, John: 'The Meaning of Silence', *Moments of Christ: The Path of Meditation* (London: Darton, Longman, and Todd, 1984).

175 Melville, Herman: *Mardi, and the Voyage Thither* (1849).

176 von Petzold, Gertrud: interviewed in 1910.

177 Channing, William Ellery: 'Christian Worship', *The Works of William E. Channing* (Boston, MA, 1846).

178 Chesterton, G.K.: 'Enjoying the Floods and Other Disasters', *The Illustrated London News*, 21 July 1906.

179 Black Elk, in *Black Elk Speaks* by John G. Neihardt (University of Nebraska Press, 1932).

180 Gilbert, Richard S.: *Harnessing Our Deepest Explosions* (1995 Essex Hall Lecture (London: The General Assembly of Unitarian and Free Christian Churches).

181 Tavkar, Ingrid: extract from *Unitarian Views of Earth and Nature* (London: General Assembly of Unitarian and Free Christian Churches, 1994).

182 Guevara, Che: quoted in *Granma* (Cuban newspaper; 1953).

183 Midgley, Celia: *Green and Dying* (London: Unitarian General Assembly Worship Committee, 1999).

184 Thich Nhat Hahn: 'A Buddhist Litany for Peace' (1976).

185 *Unitarians: Together in DIversity. A Survey of the Beliefs, Values, and Practices of Contemporary British Unitarians*, ed. Sue Woolley, p. 87 (London: The Lindsey Press, 2018).

186 *We Cannot Condemn the Flame: Poems by a Lay Buddhist.*

187 Reed, Cliff: 'Help Us To Love', *We Are Here: A Book of Prayers for Corporate Worship* (London: The Lindsey Press, 1992).

188 Elworthy, Scilla: an address given to the Oxford Unitarian congregation in February 2004.

189 Lawrence, D. H.: 'We Are Transmitters', *Pansies* (1929).

190 Ingersoll, Robert: *The Liberty of Man, Woman, and Child* (1877).

191 Quoted in *Heart to Heart: Fourteen Gatherings for Reflection and Sharing* by Christine Robinson and Alicia Hawkins (Boston: Skinner House Books, 2009; available from www.uua/bookstore).

192 Hildegard von Bingen: 'The Holy Spirit as Caritas', *Liber Divinorum Operum* (c.1172).

193 Coleridge, Samuel Taylor: 'The Rime of the Ancient Mariner', *Lyrical Ballads* (1798).

194 Usher, David: 'Come to Terms with Mortality', *Twelve Steps to Spiritual Health* (London: The Lindsey Press, 2013).

195 Eliot, George: 'The Sad Fortunes of the Rev. Amos Barton' from *Scenes of Clerical Life* (1857).

196 Wilkinson, Joan: 'Here, There, and Everywhere', *With Heart and Mind*, ed. David Dawson (London: The Worship Panel of the General Assembly of Unitarian and Free Christian Churches, 2007).

197 Thoreau, Henry: letter to Harrison Blake (20 May 1860); published in *Familiar Letters* (1865).

198 Reed, Cliff: 'Violating the Covenant', *With Heart and Mind,* ed. David Dawson (London: The Worship Panel, General Assembly of Unitarian and Free Christian Churches, 2007).

199 Plath, Sylvia: *The Unabridged Journals of Sylvia Plath* (Bantam Doubleday, 2000).

200 von Petzold, Gertrud: sermon entitled 'The Vison of Paul', *The Higher Life* (Manchester, 1908) (www.hibbbert-assembly.org.uk/ womenswork).

201 Storey, John Andrew: *The Common Quest*, eds. Charles Hughes and Sylvia Storey (London: The Lindsey Press, 2000).

202 Harley, John: 'All Souls' Day', *With Heart and Mind*, ed. David Dawson (London: The Worship Panel of the General Assembly of Unitarian and Free Christian Churches, 2007).

203 Ingersoll, Robert: quoted in *The Unitarian Life: Voices from the Past and Present*, ed. Stephen Lingwood (London: The General Assembly of Unitarian and Free Christian Churches, 2008).

204 McLachlan, John: from *The Wilderness Experience* (1994).

205 McEmrys, Aaron B.: *There is Power in Union: A Unitarian Universalist Guide to Supporting Worker Justice.* www.uua.org/sites/live-new.uua. org/files/documents/mcemrysaaron/power_union.pdf.

206 Bober, Richard: *Celebration: Another Anthology of Prayers, Meditations, and Poems by Contemporary Unitarians* (London: Unitarian Worship Subcommittee, 1998).

207 Remarque, Erich Maria: *All Quiet on the Western Front* (1929).

208 Trapp, Jacob: *Intimations of Grandeur* (London: The Lindsey Press, 1968).

209 Carruth, William Herbert: extract from 'A Firemist and a Planet', *Hymns for Living*. eds. Sydney H. Knight and David Dawson (London: The Lindsey Press, 1987).

210 Whyman, Kate: 'Introduction', *Living with Integrity: Unitarian Values and Beliefs in Practice* (London: The Lindsey Press, 2016).

211 Gibran, Kahlil: *The Prophet* (London: William Heinemann, 1926).

212 Einstein, Albert: *The Merging of Spirit and Science.*

213 Findlow, Bruce: 'A Liturgy' (c. 1975).

214 Channing, William Ellery: 'Christian Worship' (lecture, 27 July 1836).

215 Birtles, Elizabeth: 'Living the Dying', *Living with Integrity: Unitarian Values and Beliefs in Practice*, ed. Kate Whyman (London: The Lindsey Press, 2016).

216 Burns, Robert: 'To A Louse, On Seeing One on a Lady's Bonnet at Church' (1786).

217 Slee, Nicola: 'Compassion and Empowerment', a talk given at St Martin-in-the-Fields, 31 October 2011.

218 Jarvis, Jill: sermon preached in the Unitarian Universalist church of St Lawrence, 4 March 2014, http://uufl.net/sample-page-sermons/.

219 Karen Armstrong: www.charterforcompassion.org/karen-armstrong.

220 Safi, Omid (ed.): *Progressive Muslims On Justice, Gender and Pluralism* (Oxford: Oneworld, 2008).

221 Heschel, Abraham Joshua: *Who is Man?* (Stanford CA: Stanford University Press, 1965).

222 O'Donohue, John: extract from 'For the Traveller', in *Benedictus: A Book of Blessings* (London: Bantam Press, 2007).

223 Gaskell, Elizabeth: *North and South* (1855).

224 Nakashimi Brock, Rita and Parker, Rebecca Ann: *Saving Paradise: How Christianity Traded Love of This World for Crucifixion and Empire* (Boston: Beacon Press, 2009).

225 Buckminster Fuller, R.: www.brainyquote.com/quotes/r_buckminster_fuller_153429.

226 Winterson, Jeanette: *Why Be Happy When You Could Be Normal?* (London: Vintage, 2012).

227 Untitled poem from a letter to his wife, Edie Kerouac Parker, January 1957. *The Portable Jack Kerouac,* ed. Ann Charters (Penguin Classics, 2007).

228 Trapp, Jacob: *Intimations of Grandeur: Meditations by Jacob Trapp* (London: The Lindsey Press, 1968).

229 Bray McNatt, Rosemary: 'It's Hard Work', www.uua.org/worship/words/meditation/its-hard-work.

230 Davies, A. Powell: *The Language of the Heart* (New York: Farrar, Straus and Cudany, 1956).

231 Slade, Elisabeth: from an address given at New Unity Chapel, Newington Green, May 6 2018).

232 Crumbine, Nancy Jay: *Humility, Anger and Grace: Thoughts on Education and Time* (Norwich, Vermont: NorthBound Books, 2005).

233 Melville, Herman: *Mardi, and a Voyage Thither* (1849).

234 Frisk, Iain: from 'The Halsway Carol', www.bbc.co.uk/music/tracks/nzwmrb.

235 Penn, William: *Some Fruits of Solitude* (1693).

236 Fulghum, Robert: *All I Really Need to Know I Learned in Kindergarten* (Random House, 1989).

237 Davies, A. Powell: *The Language of the Heart* (New York: Farrar, Straus, and Cudahy, 1956).

238 Tinker, Sarah: in *A Circle of Seekers: A Collection of Theme Talks from Four Summer Schools (2011–2014)*, edited by Jane Blackall (Hucklow Summer School, 2015).

239 *The Poems of Emily Dickinson*, edited by R. W. Franklin (Harvard University Press, 1999).

240 Kornfield, John and Feldman, Christina: *Soul Food: Stories to Nourish the Spirit and the Heart*, San Francisco: Harper Collins (1996).

241 Thurman, Howard: *The Mood of Christmas and Other Celebrations* (1983), reprinted by Friends United Press (2011).

242 Holloway, Richard: *Between the Monster and the Saint: Reflections on the Human Condition* (Edinburgh: Canongate Books, 2008).

INDEX OF AUTHORS

A
Addison, Joseph 138
Alcott, Louisa May 33
Anonymous 9, 11, 29, 75, 145, 170, 176
Anthony, Susan B. 23, 34
Aristotle 88
Armstrong, Karen 174
Aurelius, Marcus 12, 108

B
Ballou, Hosea 134
Banbury Unitarians 115
Bartok, Béla 42
Barton, Clara 51
Barton, Jane 86
Beaudreault, Don 118
Bible, The 143, 149, 163
Birmingham Unitarians 46
Birtles, Elizabeth 172
Blair, Caroline 90
Blake, William 126
Bober, Richard 162
Boeke, Joanna 93
Boeke, Richard 25
Bowes, Jeffrey 60
Bradbury, Ray 118
Brianson, Alex 91
Brock, Rita 178
Brother Joseph Emmanuel 82
Brussatt, Frederic and Mary 121
Buddhist 34, 67, 85, 96, 99, 135, 144, 146, 159

Burnett, Frances Hodgson 141
Burns, Colleen 123
Burns, Robert 172
Burroughs, John 3, 103

C
Capek, Norbert 54, 125, 145, 157
Carruth, William Herbert 165
Carson, Rachel 110
Channing, William Ellery 48, 88, 134, 139, 167, 171
Channing, William Ellery the Younger 11
Chekov, Anton 81
Chesterton, G.K. 5, 140
Chinese, traditional 85, 109
Clarke, James Freeman 109
Coleridge, Samuel Taylor 150
Conway, Verona 39
Cromwell, Oliver 28
Crumbine, Nancy Jay 182
Curry, Michael 68
Curtis, Maria 130

D
Dadson, Michael 49
Darlison, Bill 14, 40
Davies, A. Powell 6, 23, 33, 56, 59, 69, 90, 92, 105, 115, 124, 128, 181, 186
Dawson, David 45
Dean, Kate 100
Dewey, John 112

Dickens, Charles 19
Dickinson, Emily 187
Diderot, Denis 64
Dix, Dorothea 47
Donne, John 112
Dostoyevsky, Fyodor 55
Downing, Arthur Benjamin 99
Drinkwater, John 77
Dryden, John 168
Dundas, John de 38

E

Easton, Marjorie 117
Eckhart, Meister 92
Einstein, Albert 129, 165, 167
Eliot, George 25, 79, 129, 151
Elworthy, Scilla 14, 147
Emerson, Dorothy May 3
Emerson, Ralph Waldo 12, 16,
   25, 46, 58, 66, 71, 80, 110, 116
Epictetus 6

F

Fahs, Sophia Lyon 185
Feldman, Christina 188
Findlow, Bruce 9, 115, 170
Ford, James Ishmael 1
Franciscan tradition 134
Francis of Assisi 107
Franklin, Benjamin 8
Frisk, Iain 183
Fulghum, Robert 186
Fuller, Buckminster 179
Fuller, Margaret 70

G

Gandhi, Mahatma 15, 61, 171
Gaskell, Elizabeth 4, 131, 178
Gibran, Kahlil 62, 126, 166
Gilbert, Richard S. 142
Goudge, Elizabeth 119
Grieg, Edvard 126
Griffiths, Bede 96
Guengerich, Galen 21
Guevara, Che 143

H

Hammarskjöld, Dag 76
Harley, John 158
Havel, Václav 101
Hawkins, Peter 70
Hawthorn, Nathaniel 73
Hazlitt, William 50, 103
Heisenberg, Weiner 101
Heschel, Abraham 176
Hildegard of Bingen 150
Hindu tradition 40, 59, 94, 105,
   113, 139
Hodges, Steve 41
Holloway, Richard 189
Howe, Anthony 19, 31

I

Ingersoll, Robert 66, 148, 158

J

Jarvis, Jill 174
Jefferson, Thomas 51
Jewish tradition 46, 69, 103
Johnson, Penny 47

K
Keane, Feargal 119
Keip, Margaret 40
Keller, Helen 89
Kereki, Gábor 161
Kerouac, Jack 180
King, Martin Luther Jr 7, 36, 53
Kipling, Rudyard 82
Knght, Sydney 114
Kornfield, John 188

L
Lamb, Charles 21
Larson, Philip 84
Law, William 77
Lawrence, D.H. 148
Levi, Primo 13
Lingwood, Stephen 45
Longfellow, Henry Wadsworth 97
Lovis, Richard 87, 123
Luther, Martin 162

M
MacDonald, Claire 155, 184
Main, John 136
Mandela, Nelson 9, 21
Martineau, James 55
Mason, Leonard 82
McAuley, Derek 54
McEmrys, Aaron B. 160
McCready, Tom 54, 120
McLachlan, John 159
McNatt, Rosemary Bray 181
McNeile, Tony 155
Melville, Herman 137, 183
Midgley, Celia 144
Monk, David 27, 61

Montaigne, Michel de 78, 177
Montesquieu, Charles de 30
Morgan, Peggy 35
Muslim tradition 17, 44

N
Naish, John 79
Native American tradition 41, 81, 141, 160, 169, 175
Newman, Francis William 72
Nightingale, Florence 65, 113

O
Obama, Barack 125
O'Donohue, John 177

P
Paine, Thomas 20
Pakula, Andrew 47
Parker, Rebecca 178
Parker, Theodore 28, 64
Parks, Rosa 18
Pauling, Linus 117
Penn, William 22, 184
Petzold, Gertrud von 98, 138, 154
Plath, Sylvia 153
Price, Robert McNair 39
Priestley, Joseph 37, 176

R
Ratushinskaya, Irina 37
Reed, Cliff 2, 24, 43, 65, 147, 153
Reeve, Christopher 136
Remarque, Erich Maria 163
Rogers (Birtles), Elizabeth 109
Rohr, Richard 120

Roy, Raja Ram Mohun 137
Ruskin, John 83

S
Sackville-West, Vita 164
Safi, Omid 174
Sandburg, Carl 101
Sarum Primer 7
Schweitzer, Albert 7, 42, 48, 84, 127
Seccombe, Josephine 71, 104
Seeger, Pete 61
Short, Harry Lismer 2, 57, 83, 106, 111
Sikh tradition 100
Slade, Elizabeth 182
Slee, Nicola 173
Smart, Christopher 51
Smith, Matthew 13
Spong, John Shelby 44
Stevenson, Adlai 18, 72
Storey, John Andrew 4, 29, 154
Sufi tradition 8, 17, 27, 28, 43, 73, 86, 101

T
Tagore, Rabindranath 102
Taoist tradition 111, 132
Tarbox, Elizabeth 4
Tarfon, Rabbi 5
Tavkar, Ingrid 142
Thomas, Edward 89
Thomas, Gospel of 94
Thoreau, Henry 30, 62, 67, 78, 152, 169
Thurman, Howard 188
Thursfield, Alison 31
Tinker, Sarah 95, 187

Toye, John 58
Traherne, Thomas 35, 68, 80
Trapp, Jacob 15, 26, 32, 38, 56, 95, 108, 122, 164, 180
Tutu, Desmond 17, 70, 104

U
Underhill, Evelyn 133
Usher, David 10, 32, 57, 66, 74, 131, 151

V
Vogt, Von Ogden 26
Voltaire 168
Vonnegut, Kurt 50

W
Walker, Frank 53, 63, 132
Walsh, Robert 97, 136
Weil, Simone 127
Whitman, Walt 63, 93
Whyman, Kate 166
Wilkins, Howard 130
Wilkinson, Joan 152
Williamson, Marianne 121
Winterson, Jeanette 179
Wittenburg, Jonathan 52
Wollstonecraft, Mary 36, 128
Wright, Frank Lloyd 50

Y
York, Sarah 22
Yousafzai, Malala 76

Z
Zoroastrian tradition 20

CPSIA information can be obtained
at www.ICGtesting.com
Printed in the USA
BVHW071023020519
547195BV00001B/23/P

9 780853 190912